Plays of Belonging
Three Plays by Rex Deverell

BELONGING • WEIRD KID • VIDEO WARS

Playwrights Canada Press
Toronto • Canada

Plays of Belonging - Three Plays by Rex Deverell © 1997
Belonging © 1996 *Weird Kid* © 1996 *Video Wars* © 1996
Playwrights Canada Press
54 Wolseley St., 2nd fl. Toronto, Ontario CANADA M5T 1A5
Tel: (416) 703-0201 Fax: (416) 703-0059
e-mail: cdplays@interlog.com   http://www.puc.ca

CAUTION: These plays are fully protected under the copyright laws of Canada and all other countries of The Copyright Union, and are subject to royalty. Changes to the scripts are expressly forbidden without the prior written permission of the author. Rights to produce, film, or record, in whole or in part, in any medium or any language, by any group, *amateur or professional*, are retained by the author. Those interested in obtaining amateur production rights please contact Playwrights Union of Canada (PUC). The playwright administers the professional production rights, please contact PUC for further information.

No part of this book, covered by the copyright hereon, may be reproduced or used in any form or by any means - graphic, electronic or mechanical - without the prior written permission of the *publisher* except for excerpts in a review. Any request for photocopying, recording, taping or information storage and retrieval systems of any part of this book shall be directed in writing to The Canadian Copyright Licensing Agency, 6 Adelaide Street East, Suite 900, Toronto, Ontario CANADA M5C 1H6 tel: (416) 868-1620.

Playwrights Canada Press publishes with the generous assistance of The Canada Council for the Arts - Writing and Publishing Section, and the Ontario Arts Council.

Cover and interior illustrations by Shelton Deverell.

Canadian Cataloguing in Publication Data
Deverell, Rex, 1941 —
        Plays of belonging : three plays
ISBN 0-88754-531-9
I. Title.
PS8557.B877P52   1997   C812'.54   C97-930302-8
PR9199.3.D48P52   1997

First edition: August, 1997.
Printed and bound in Winnipeg, Manitoba, Canada - Hignell Printing Ltd.

Contents

Introduction	p. 9
Belonging	p. 13
Weird Kid	p. 59
Video Wars	p. 101

Rex Deverell was born in Toronto, raised in Orillia, rooted in the Prairies (Regina), uprooted and now lives in Toronto. He set a record for the greatest number of years as playwright-in-residence in a Canadian theatre — Globe Theatre, 1975-1990.

He has, on occasion, served time in various offices of playwrights' organisations, including president of the Playwrights Union of Canada.

Dedicated to all those who have ever felt like strangers in a strange place.

Special thanks to:

Sharon Enkin, Emily Hearn, Ken Kramer, Rina Singh, the Pizza Group, and my family - Rita and Shelton, all of whom helped with research or as sounding boards.

R.J.D.

Introduction

When I first ran across Rex Deverell's plays in the summer of 1988, I realized I had come across a body of work that would strike a chord with young people. It challenged conventional ideas and engaged its audience in a search for solutions to every kid's daily trials and tribulations. As I read through plays like "The Underground Lake", "Melody Meets the Bag Lady", "The Copetown City Kite Crisis" and "Weird Kid", I kept hearing the voices of young people exploring the world around them.

In "The Underground Lake" Rex sets up a universal situation of uneasy dependency not unlike the Arab-Israeli relationship or that of Quebec within the rest of Canada, where people must look past the rhetoric of hatred in order to live in peace and co-operation. In "Melody Meets the Bag Lady" we are made to wonder who has the right to try to shape the lives of old people. Is it the sympathetic hand-outs of government programmes? Is it the well-intentioned relative or individual? In "The Copetown City Kite Crisis" he asks his audience to take a vote on whether making the greatest kite in the world is worth polluting the local air and water. In "Weird Kid" he shows us how easy it is to blame others and how difficult it can be to take responsibility for our own bad behaviour. In each case he is asking the audience to participate in the search for the right thing to do.

I decided to find Rex to ask him for the rights to perform "Copetown". I was surprised to find that he had recently re-located to the East End of Toronto.

A year later, the Founding Director of the Golden Horseshoe Players, Sharon Enkin, asked Rex to write a play that dealt with the issue of violence in the media, and whether children were being subjected to too much violence on TV and through computer games. It was a time when Mortal Kombat converged with the Persian Gulf War.

Rex wanted, as always, to get the true voice of young people at the time. Were they excited by violence? Yes they were. Shocking, but real. Rex writes into "Video Wars" the dichotomy between the attraction of war, with its sounds of gunfire and bombs dropping, and the brutal reality of the families and loved ones torn apart by it. The message has to be brought home to Canadian kids far removed from the violence of war in an honest and believable way. Rex does it with emotion and caring and even a touch of humour.

The Golden Horseshoe Players also asked Rex to write something for an older audience on the theme of violence against women. His play, "Short Circuit" was nominated for a Chalmers Award for writing in 1994.

We then asked him to write about literacy, because we had successfully toured a British play in the early 80's about the importance of keeping reading and story-telling alive. Rex came up with "Belonging" in 1995, a play that shows the anguish of misunderstood youth, written in beautiful poetry that is packed with a mix of frustration and hope. The special thing about Rex's plays is that he understands the importance of having every word and emotion ring true. Young people are the toughest to win over — they immediately recognize any false word, action or intention. They bridle at preachiness. Rex always researches how his potential audience walks and talks. He tries out his dialogue in classrooms before submitting his work. And then he finds ways to draw his audiences into the conflict, by reflecting different sides of themselves through his characters — some empathetic, some questionable in their motivations. This is Rex Deverell's strength as a playwright — his ability to not just tell good stories but to engage an audience in determining the outcome of the conflicts that he sets up. When the members of the Chalmers Award committee of the Ontario Arts Council saw "Belonging" in 1996 they felt what it was like to be drawn into a Rex Deverell play, through his use of language, colourful and disturbing imagery, and personal self-examination that are the hallmarks of his work. They appreciated that he was able to get inside the heads of young people to have them work through the problems facing them, in a way that was honest and forthright. That's why they gave him the award for Writing for Young Audiences in May of 1996.

The Golden Horseshoe Players are very proud to have had the opportunity to commission two of these three fine works from one of Canada's best playwrights. His work continues to force audiences to examine the world around them and to try to piece together how they can best deal with some of the difficult issues facing them today. His plays are meant to be unsettling, because discovering the right answer often means facing the hard realities of how people treat one another. Rex Deverell sees with a piercing unyielding eye and speaks worlds of meaning through the honest voices of his young characters.

Bruce Griffin
Artistic Director
Golden Horseshoe Players
July, 1997

Belonging

Playwright's Introduction

What happens to a child who has a talent and because of this very gift is rejected by her school mates? That question was where I began and the whole play flowed from that question. *Belonging* was the third play the Golden Horseshoe Players asked me to write for them. It brought me back to the child who doesn't fit in — the subject of *Weird Kid*, a play from my Globe Theatre days. But this time it is a child who wants so much to belong that she is willing to give up the thing she enjoys most, the thing that makes her most herself.

There are two great things about *Belonging* if I do say so myself. Kids identify with Jody. After every show children put up their hands to tell us how they felt when they came to a new school. And the second thing is that it inspired poetry!

Sue Miner directed. She had acted in some of my plays in Saskatchewan and has become an accomplished director in her own right. She brought just the right combination of the child-like and the artful to the play.

Belonging received its first performance January 23, 1995 at Percy W. Merry Public School, Hornby, Ontario (Halton School Board) with the following cast:

Lindsey Connell
Brian Elliott
Xavier MacDonald
Heidi Verwey

Director - Sue Miner.
Stage manager - Jennifer Stobart.

CHARACTERS

JODY	The poet artist child - who may get to be a great genius if she survives childhood. Age 10 or 11.
CRYSTAL DELISLE	Crystal is destined to become the prom queen when she gets to high school. She's bright but her frame of reference is narrow. Age 10 or 11.
ALAN LOW	He seems to be struggling to keep up with the class. He is a natural follower — going along with things is the easiest course for him. Age 10.
TEACHER	(Mr. Beantree) He is trying to deal with a behavioural problem but realizes that there is a genius at work in his class. He is caught between the need for discipline and the need not to squelch genuine creativity.
MOTHER	(Normally would be played by the same performer who plays CRYSTAL) Jody's mother. A bright woman with a new job in a new city.
FATHER	(Normally would double with ALAN) Jody's father, Jace. He also is getting used to a new position with creative challenges.

BELONGING

Scene: a space which can become a classroom, a child's bedroom, a kitchen, a playground — almost instantly. (The first production utilized a thrust stage with risers of various sizes and a chalkboard flat upstage) At the beginning of the play the room is a classroom.

JODY enters from the audience and appraises the room.

JODY: This can be my school, okay? My new school and this is my very first day. And — and (*pointing to one of the audience members*) you...

ACTOR: Who me?

JODY: Yeah. You can be the teacher, Mr... Mr. Beantree, okay?!

ACTOR: (*coming to the front*) Sure.

JODY: And you (*getting another audience member*) be one of the kids — Crystal — and she's kind of stuck up, sort of?

ACTRESS: (*striking a pose*) Like this?

JODY: Right! (*picking out another actor*) And you can be Alan. He's another kid. (*to the audience*) And you can be the rest of the class. (*to CRYSTAL and ALAN*) So you guys are fooling around and I try to play with you.

CRYSTAL	Alright.

CRYSTAL and ALAN enter, playing Follow the Leader.

JODY	... and Mr. Beantree hasn't come in yet so you wait there...

JODY tries to play with them.

Okay, Teacher.

TEACHER enters suddenly.

TEACHER	Good morning, class.
STUDENTS	Good morning, Mr. Beantree.
TEACHER	(*indicating a place for JODY*) That will be your desk...
JODY	Jody.
TEACHER	That will be your desk, Jody.
JODY	(*sitting down*) Thanks...
TEACHER	We have a new student with us this morning. (*to JODY, smiling*) Stand up, Jody. (*to class*) Her name is Jody Maxwell. Say hello, class.
STUDENTS	Hello, Jody.
JODY	Hi!
TEACHER	Jody has just moved to the city. She doesn't know anyone — right, Jody?
JODY	Right.
TEACHER	I bet things are feeling a little strange.

JODY	A little.
TEACHER	However, this is a very friendly school — (*to the class*) isn't it, boys and girls?
STUDENTS	Yes, Mr. Beantree.
TEACHER	And I'm sure we will all want to be helpful and make Jody feel welcome, won't we?
STUDENTS	Yes, Mr. Beantree.
TEACHER	Very good. Now — Jody, why don't you tell us about yourself.
JODY	Alright...
TEACHER	We would all be interested in that, wouldn't we, class?
STUDENTS	Yes, Mr. Beantree.
JODY	Great!

Everyone looks at JODY for a moment. She shrinks a little.

TEACHER	Take a deep breath and speak in a big voice, Jody,
JODY	Okay, (*pausing*)

I grew up in a little tiny town
way, way up north.
In the summer the sun shines almost the whole night long
In the winter there are curtains of light in the sky
Most people speak another language that sounds like wind rushing through trees
Or water gurgling under the ice.

There is snickering among the students.

TEACHER   Children...

                Temporary silence.

JODY   (*plunging on*) And there are no sidewalks or roads hardly,
                Just grass or snow or rocks
                And sometimes school closes down and the whole town goes moose hunting or goose hunting—

                Laughter.

                — and — what do you want to know?

TEACHER   Would anyone like to ask Jody a question?

                CRYSTAL puts up her hand.

                Crystal?

CRYSTAL   Are there any shopping malls up there?

JODY   Shopping malls? Are you kidding?

CRYSTAL   Boring.

TEACHER   Any other questions?

                Total silence.

TEACHER   Well, thank you, Jody,

                She sits down.

                Now, class, we are going to start the morning with a brand new unit in English and our subject is: (*writing on the board*) "The power of poetry"

JODY   (*enthusiastic*) Yay!

TEACHER	... and our first assignment of the day is to write a poem. Who can give me an example of a poem.
CRYSTAL	(*waving her hand*) Oh, I can! I can!
TEACHER	Yes, Crystal Delisle.
CRYSTAL	Baa baa black sheep, have you any wool—
TEACHER	Yes, nursery rhymes are poems...
CRYSTAL	Yes sir, yes sir — three bags full.
TEACHER	Thank you, Crystal.
CRYSTAL	One for the master...
TEACHER	Yes, yes — that's fine.

JODY giggles.

CRYSTAL	(*scowling*) What's so funny?

JODY doesn't reply.

TEACHER:	Alan Low.
ALAN	I didn't do anything.
TEACHER	I didn't say you did. Now, Alan. What is it about a nursery rhyme that makes it a poem?
ALAN	I don't know.
TEACHER	Come on, Alan. Corral those horses. What is it about a nursery rhyme that makes it a poem?
CRYSTAL	I know, I know.
TEACHER	Yes, Crystal?

CRYSTAL   Certain words sound the same?

TEACHER   That's right. They... they sound the same, "any *wool*, three bags *full*"
Wool - full.
Wool-full...

JODY giggles again.

Jody? What are you laughing at?

JODY   Woolfull.

TEACHER   Wool full?

JODY   Woolfull. It's funny!

TEACHER   (*not amused*) Now, another thing that poems have...

JODY   Awfully woolful,

TEACHER   Another thing that...

JODY   Woofully awful,

TEACHER   Another...

JODY   Woefully woolful...

TEACHER   Jody.

She is quiet.

Poems also have rhythm — rhythm — like drums — bump bumpity bump bumpity bump bumpity...

JODY is careful not to laugh.

TEACHER	"I must go down to the sea again The lonely sea and the sky..." Or a dance — (*limerick rhythm*) Deyadahdah — dahdahdah... (*he dances about*) Deyadadadada (*etc.*)

JODY cannot contain herself.

Jody.

JODY	Yes, Sir.
TEACHER	A student who acts like a fool Better learn this one little rule Put your hand up And don't interrupt Or I'll make you stay after school

The TEACHER is pleased with himself.

Now that is a poem. That sort of poem is called a—

JODY	Limerick?
CRYSTAL	Shhh. (*scoffing*) Limrik, hah!
TEACHER	Yes, actually. A limerick.
CRYSTAL	I knew that. (*she didn't*)
JODY	Sorry, Sir.
TEACHER	Rhyme, rhythm and what else?

Silence.

Git yer thinkin' caps on, pardners. (*MR. BEANTREE likes to put on a character from time to time*) Get those wagons a-rollin'!

JODY   Feelings?

TEACHER   (*exasperated*) I don't know what your old school was like—

JODY   Really tiny!

TEACHER   But in this school we put up our hand when we want to speak. Understood?

JODY nods.

Good.

He turns his attention back to the class.

Rhyme, rhythm and ...? Come on, people! It's as plain as the nose on your face.

ALAN   (*putting his hand up*) Your mouth?

TEACHER   What comes out of your mouth, Alan?

ALAN   Spit?

CRYSTAL   I know, I know.

TEACHER   Crystal?

CRYSTAL   Words?

TEACHER   Yes, yes! That's what I was looking for! Words! Poetry is made up of words but not just ordinary words — wonderful words — words that sing and dance and are full of power — the power of poetry! Alright, class — a little exercise. I am as happy as... Come on — finish my sentence. I am as happy as... Alan?

ALAN   How am I supposed to know how happy you are?

TEACHER	No — no — how happy are you?
ALAN	Not very.
TEACHER	I am as happy as ... a what?
JODY	A lizard?
OTHERS	Hahahahaha
TEACHER	A lizard?
JODY	Yep.
TEACHER	Yes, Mr. Beantree.
JODY	Yes, Mr. Beantree.
TEACHER	But why is a lizard happy?
JODY	Well, I don't know about most lizards but this one is happy because — because he can fly!
TEACHER	(*dubiously*) Alright. Anyone else. I am as happy as...

Both ALAN and CRYSTAL have their hands up.

Alan?

He puts his down.

Crystal?

CRYSTAL	A new dress.
ALAN	(*waving his hand*) I know! I know!
TEACHER	Alan?

Pause.

TEACHER	I am as happy as...?
ALAN	I forgot.
TEACHER	Well, never mind. Now that we are all warmed up, get out your pencils, everybody, and write down all the words you can think of. Come on, hurry up. Now, choose the best ones and make a poem.

The students get busy.

Put your hand up when you have finished.

In a few seconds, CRYSTAL puts her hand up.

Very good, Crystal.

ALAN	Sir?
TEACHER	Yes, Alan?
ALAN	I can't think of anything.
TEACHER	Saddle the bronco, there, Alan, and hitch up the old brain.
ALAN	(*muttering*) Hitch up the...
TEACHER	The brain.
ALAN	Yes, Sir.

JODY puts her hand up.

TEACHER	You, too, Jody.
JODY	I'm finished.
TEACHER	Oh. Well, very good. Alright. Time's up. Let's hear yours, Crystal. Listen carefully, class.

CRYSTAL   I am a very nice girl
               I wear my hair in a curl—

ALAN   No she doesn't.

TEACHER   Shhh.

CRYSTAL   I have a new dress
               It is one of the best
               And makes me look really nice.

               Pause.

               I couldn't get the last word to —

TEACHER   Rhyme.

JODY   More or less? More or less rhymes with dress.

TEACHER   It was a very good try, Crystal.

CRYSTAL   Thank you.

TEACHER   Now, Jody. Let the class hear your poem.

               JODY is totally involved in the world of her poem.

JODY   One day I saw a lizard
               Flying around in the sky
               It had scaly leathery wings
               That flapped and flopped
               Then it landed
               Right beside my big toe.
               I bent down
               And it whispered to me
               With a sleazy slimy slithering sound
               "What are you doing
               Crawling around
               Here on the ground."

>   *There is a moment of stunned silence and then:*

CRYSTAL   A flying lizard! Hahaha/hahaahahahaa!

ALAN   (*overlapping at the / in CRYSTAL's line above*) Her big toe! Hahahaha!

CRYSTAL   What a funny girl!

ALAN   What a funny girl!

TOGETHER   Hahahaha!

CRYSTAL   Mr. Beantree. Mr. Beantree? That's not a poem is it? It doesn't even rhyme hardly.

TEACHER   Well, Crystal, some poems rhyme and some poems don't. This one doesn't and it's very good. Jody.

JODY   (*pleased with herself*) Yes, Sir?

TEACHER   Where did you get that poem, Jody?

JODY   (*in a small shattered voice*) I made it up.

TEACHER   I beg your pardon?

JODY   I made it up myself.

TEACHER   Let me see.

>   *He looks through her papers and sees she has made it up herself.*

I'm sorry. Of course you made it up yourself. It was — it sounded like it had been written by a real poet — I mean someone who — I'm sorry. (*pause*) Jody?

> *Pause.*

JODY	Yes, Mr. Beantree?
TEACHER	I'm sorry.
JODY	Yes, Mr. Beantree.
TEACHER	You don't feel hurt, do you?
JODY	No, Mr. Beantree.
TEACHER	It was a mistake.
JODY	Yes, Mr. Beantree.
OTHERS	(*mocking*) Yes, Mr. Beantree. No, Mr. Beantree.
TEACHER	(*not knowing what else to do he tries to get back to the lesson*) Poetry — wonderful words that...

JODY puts her hand up.

(*suddenly happy*) Ah, Jody! Do you have a question?

JODY	May I please go to the washroom?

Snickering from the others.

TEACHER	(*warning*) Class. (*as they settle down, wearily*) Yes, Jody. You may go to the washroom.
CRYSTAL	Look, she's got ducks on her blue jeans.

JODY does indeed have pictures of ducks on her jeans — in felt appliqué, a native design that might have been crafted in the North.

ALAN	Little ducky wuckies.

JODY gets up and leaves the class.

JODY (*to audience*) I thought this school would be a fun place. Why does the teacher keep on asking me questions. And those kids — why do they keep on laughing at me? I love these jeans. Everybody in my school wore jeans like these. I don't know what to do! (*pause*) I know what I'll do. I'll go home. And I won't eat any supper and I'll go to bed early and maybe when I wake up in the morning — I'll find out it was all just a bad dream.

To ALAN and CRYSTAL, if they are doubling as the parents.

Okay, you guys be my Mom and Dad now.

She goes to sleep. ALAN and CRYSTAL become her parents. Sound of an alarm clock.

MOTHER (*off*) Jody. Jody! Time to get ready for school, dear.

JODY It wasn't just a bad dream.

She moans and pulls the covers over her head.

MOTHER Jody! You don't want to be late!

JODY (*calling*) I can't, Mom.

MOTHER (*entering*) What's that, dear?

JODY I can't go to school.

MOTHER Why not? (*she puts a hand to JODY's forehead*) You aren't sick.

JODY I'm not?

MOTHER Nope.

JODY There's no school today.

MOTHER	There isn't?
JODY	It's a — a — P-Day. Yeah. That's what it is.
MOTHER	A P-Day?
JODY	Yeah.
MOTHER	What's a P-Day?
JODY	Where the teachers go to school and the kids stay at home.
MOTHER	Professional development.
JODY	Right. P —
MOTHER	D.
JODY	Day.
MOTHER	Strange.
JODY	What?
MOTHER	They usually let us know.
JODY	I — I forgot.
MOTHER	Oh, Jody! How am I going to do this? I have to go to work — (*calling*) Jace?
FATHER	(*calling*) Yeah?
MOTHER	Can you stay home today?
FATHER	I can't hear you. The water's running.
MOTHER	Well, turn it off then.

FATHER	What?
MOTHER	Turn it off.

FATHER shows up in his bathrobe and drying hair.

FATHER	I couldn't hear you.
MOTHER	Can you work at home?
FATHER	Why?
MOTHER	Jody doesn't have any school today.
FATHER	Since when?
MOTHER	She forgot the notice.
JODY	I'm sorry.
MOTHER	Can you, Jace? I've got appointments all morning.
FATHER	I'll have to phone. You're sure about this, Jody?

Pause.

Jody?

Pause.

Jody, are you sure about it?

BOTH stare at JODY.

JODY	Don't make me go to that school. Please.
MOTHER	You don't usually lie to us, Jody.

	Silence.
FATHER	What's wrong?
JODY	Nothing.
FATHER	Cornflakes?
JODY	Yes, please.

They mime eating breakfast.

	Nobody likes me.
FATHER	(*too quickly*) I'm sure that's not true —
MOTHER	Somebody must like you —
JODY	They think I'm funny.
FATHER	What's wrong with that, Munchkin? What's wrong with being funny?
JODY	They laugh at me, Dad! Back home...
MOTHER	This is home now, Jody.
JODY	I know, you explained it to me — but at my old school everybody was nice — sort of. And here everybody looks different and talks different and then they look at me like I'm the weird one.
FATHER	It's just because you're new. Give them a few days.
MOTHER	You'll make friends, you'll see.
JODY	How?
FATHER	Tell them how great they are. Everybody likes people who think they're great.

MOTHER	And maybe you should — I don't know — (*looking at her watch*) try to fit in.
JODY	But you always tell me to be myself.
MOTHER	To be yourself. I know — but —
FATHER	And you're great!
MOTHER	But just until they get used to you, okay?
JODY	Okay.
FATHER	Okay.
MOTHER	Run and get ready.
JODY	Can I wear a dress?
MOTHER	A dress?
JODY	Yes, a dress.
MOTHER	This is a first! Why?
JODY	(*on her way*) Crystal.
FATHER	(*to MOTHER*) Crystal?
JODY	(*off*) Crystal wears dresses.

> *MOTHER shrugs. TEACHER enters and the scene reverts to the classroom. PARENTS revert to CRYSTAL and ALAN. CRYSTAL is wearing jeans. JODY enters wearing a dress — sees Crystal's jeans and reacts.*

JODY	You've got jeans on!
CRYSTAL	So?

JODY	They're — they're nice.

JODY sits down at her desk.

TEACHER	Good morning, class.
CLASS	Good morning, Mr. Beantree.
TEACHER	Did you all remember your homework?
CRYSTAL & ALAN	Yes, Mr. Beantree.
TEACHER	And what was that, class?
CLASS	Write another poem.
TEACHER	So, first of all — perhaps Jody would read hers to the class. I just want you to listen to what a wonderful poet Jody is.

JODY doesn't move.

Jody?

JODY	I couldn't think of anything.
TEACHER	(*disappointed*) Are you sure?
JODY	Yes, sir.
TEACHER	Very well. Alan?
ALAN	(*very fast*) I hate to do my homework Because it's too much work.
TEACHER	Pardon?
ALAN	I hate to do my homework Because it's too much work.

TEACHER   That's it?

ALAN   Yup.

CRYSTAL   Hahahaahah.

JODY   Hahahahaha.

CRYSTAL gives her an odd look.

TEACHER   That'll be enough of that.

ALAN   (*to JODY*) Least I had a poem.

TEACHER   Crystal, would you like to read us your poem?

CRYSTAL   This poem is called "Things I Like".

Things I Like — by Crystal Delisle.

There are a lot of things I like
Because they are a delight.
I like my blue jeans
Which my mother presses and cleans.
I think Mr. Beantree is neat
Being in school is such a treat.

Thank you.

TEACHER   Thank you, Crystal.

CRYSTAL   You're welcome.

TEACHER   You may sit down now.

CRYSTAL   Oh. (*she does*)

TEACHER   Now, class — what did you think of Crystal's poem. Alan?

ALAN	It was okay.
JODY	(*overly enthusiastic*) I thought it was wonderful!
TEACHER	(*surprised*) You did? Why?
JODY	It was so — it was so — so cute.

Bell rings.

TEACHER	Recess time.

Everybody is in sudden motion. JODY starts towards CRYSTAL.

JODY	Crystal — I just wanted to...

CRYSTAL brushes past her towards ALAN.

CRYSTAL	Alan — did you really think my poem was okay?
ALAN	Want to play catch?
JODY	Wait, I just wanted to...

CRYSTAL and ALAN go off together.

...to tell you how great you are.

(*to the audience*) Actually I did make up a poem last night. It's just that I couldn't read it to the class. If they think I'm weird now — listen to this.

As she reads, the rest of the cast act it out.

(*imitating CRYSTAL*) My poem is called "Somewhere a Roaring Giant" (*viciously*) ... by Jody.

Somewhere a roaring giant roams
Nobody's safe in their homes

He towers and glowers
And stomps through the flowers
He tramps on those poor tiny trembly things
With their little see-through wings
They hide in the grass hoping he'll pass
And miss them as they hide in the grass.
Watch out, Alan and Crystal and Mr. Beantree
The monster is coming to eat you three
He's getting closer and closer
And he's getting grosser and grosser.
Who is the giant who is so mad?
Who would crumble a house and be glad?
Who would sit on a school if he could
Until it was nothing but splinters of wood?
Who is this monster who'd pick up a kid
And throw her around like a garbage can lid?
Who is this beast grinning and scowling
Filling the air with his terrible howling?
Come close and I'll tell you
I'll whisper who
I'm the monster, don't you see?
The monster is me.

I feel so mad I could hit somebody!

> *ALAN races by and grabs the poem out of her hand.*

Hey! That's mine. Give me that!

> *She takes off after him.*

ALAN   Come and get it, Dodo Bird!

CRYSTAL   Give it to me! Give it to me!

JODY   No fair! You don't do that when somebody makes something. You don't mess it up!

ALAN   Who says?

The TEACHER enters.

TEACHER No fighting! I said no fighting. Alright — that will be after school for all three of you. I'll take that. (*retrieving the poem which is by now in pieces*) Thank you very much. Now, into the classroom.

The children exit. The TEACHER's shoulders slump. He crumples up the pieces of paper and absently puts them in his pocket and exits. JODY enters.

JODY I hate it here! What am I going to do? Maybe I should run away. Yeah. I'll leave a little note for my parents — Dear Mom and Dad — sorry I'm so much trouble. Good bye forever. Your sweet little girl, Jody. I'll set my alarm clock...

Clock alarm sounds.

...to ring in the middle of the night.. Gosh it's dark. I'll climb out of my window. (*banging her knee*) Ow. Gosh it's cold. Maybe I'd better go back and get my sweater. Ow! Maybe I should get my teddy bear, too. And I could take my fuzzy slippers. No. I won't take my fuzzy slippers. Maybe I should make myself a peanut butter sandwich in case I get hungry — or a bologna sandwich. What if it rains? What if there's thunder and lightning? What if I get lost? What if a bad guy grabs me? Maybe I should — maybe I should — I should...

She goes to sleep. Ghostly shapes surround the bed.

CRYSTAL What a funny girl!

ALAN What a funny girl!

TEACHER	If you act like a fool I'll make you stay in after school!
CRYSTAL	After school...
ALAN	After school, Dodo Bird!
TEACHER	Where did you get this poem, Jody?
JODY	(*in her sleep*) I made it up!
CRYSTAL	Made it up!
ALAN	Gimme that!
CRYSTAL	Gimme that!
TEACHER	Gimme that!
JODY	(*struggling*) No, no, no!

The shapes disappear.

JODY Don't take my poems away! (*sitting upright in bed*) I want to go home! (*looking around*) Oh. Just a bad dream. (*snuggling back*) This time.

MOTHER (*off*) Time to get up, Jody! Time for school.

FATHER (*off*) Wakey, wakey, rise and shine!

He imitates a bugle playing "Reveille".

JODY (*disgusted*) Dad!

He stops.

I should have run away.

The telephone rings.

MOTHER   Jace! Will you get that?

FATHER   What?

MOTHER   Get the phone.

FATHER   I can't hear you. The water is running. (*pause*) Is anybody going to get that phone?

He emerges in his bathrobe,

Do I have to do everything around here?

MOTHER   I've got eggs on the stove.

FATHER   I'm getting it.

MOTHER   Who is it?

FATHER   Wait a minute. Wait a minute.

He picks up the telephone. Immediately we see the TEACHER on the other end of the line.

Yes?

TEACHER   May I speak to Mr. or Mrs. Maxwell?

FATHER   Jace Maxwell here.

TEACHER   This is Henry Beantree. (*pause*) Jody's teacher?

FATHER   Ah!

MOTHER   Who is it?

FATHER   The teacher!

MOTHER looks at JODY, who is terrified. They join FATHER at the telephone.

TEACHER   Sorry to call so early...

FATHER   (*drying his hair*) No problem.

        MOTHER may try to serve him some toast.

TEACHER   I — I don't know how to put this but...Did Jody tell you what happened at school yesterday?

FATHER   (*with a look at JODY*) What happened at school? Not unless she told her mother?

        MOTHER shakes her head. JODY shrugs.

TEACHER   Oh. (*pause*)

MOTHER   What happened?

FATHER   What happened?

TEACHER   Oh, a little problem in the school yard. I've been a little worried about her, Mr. Maxwell.

FATHER   Worried?

TEACHER   I wondered if you and Jody's mother might have time to come in and see me.

FATHER   What about this morning?

TEACHER   Terrific. I'll look forward to it.

FATHER   Us too.

TEACHER   Good-bye.

        They hang up, TEACHER exits, JODY's parents turn to her.

JODY   Uh...

FATHER	Yes?
JODY	I...
MOTHER	Yes?
JODY	Uh... But...if...uh...
PARENTS	Yes?
JODY	Could we go back up North? (*running off*)
MOTHER	Jody!

She and FATHER exit following JODY.

JODY	(*popping out and addressing the audience*) So here is what happened when my parents came to visit my teacher.

TEACHER sits as if at his desk. MOTHER and FATHER arrive. TEACHER rises to greet them. The backslash - / - indicates the beginning of the next line. The two speeches overlap at this point.

TEACHER	Ah, Mr. and Mrs. Maxwell...
MOTHER	/Linda.
FATHER	Jace.
TEACHER	Henry. It was so good of you to come — I'm sure you are very busy.
FATHER	/No, not at all...
MOTHER	Well, kind of — but /not when it comes to Jody.
FATHER	Not when it comes to Jody.

TEACHER	Please, sit down, sit down. May I get you some coffee?
FATHER	/Had my quota.
MOTHER	No, thank you.
TEACHER	Isn't it a nice day?
FATHER	/Beautiful.
MOTHER	Very nice.
TEACHER	So how are you liking the city? Big change, I guess —
FATHER	/Big change.
MOTHER	Quite a change from up North.
FATHER	New /jobs —
MOTHER	New people. A little hard at first —
FATHER	Getting /used to things.
MOTHER	Getting used to it.

Pause.

PARENTS	(*together*) Jody.
TEACHER	Jody.
JODY	(*from the side*) Finally.
TEACHER	Well, Jody is having a little trouble getting used to it too.
MOTHER	Yes?

TEACHER	She has become very quiet.
FATHER	Quiet?
TEACHER	She hardly says a word in class. She started off — well...bouncy and happy. But that stopped and she was writing poems too, but that stopped...
FATHER	Stopped writing poetry?
JODY	They just make me sound weird.
MOTHER	I told her to try to fit in. Wrong?
TEACHER	Probably. I made a big mistake myself — the very first day.
JODY	(*imitating him*) Where did you get that poem, Jody?
TEACHER	I told her I didn't think she had written her own poem.
FATHER	Ah.
JODY	I'm never going to write a another poem as long as I live.
MOTHER	We thought the city would be so good for her.
JODY	Thanks a lot.
TEACHER	And then yesterday in the school yard — well she was fighting.
MOTHER	Not our Jody!
TEACHER	Something was taken from her and she was so angry — I was afraid she was going to hurt someone.
JODY	I would have, too.

TEACHER	I can't have children hurting each other in my class.
FATHER	Of /course not.
MOTHER	No. Certainly.
TEACHER	She could get expelled.
PARENTS	(*stunned*) What?
TEACHER	Policy of the School Board. Zero Fighting.
JODY	But they took my poem.
MOTHER	But she's just a little girl.
TEACHER	Zero fighting. Fight and you get kicked right out of the school.
JODY	And they ripped it up!
FATHER	Was it all Jody's fault?
TEACHER	No, of course not...
JODY	That's for sure.
TEACHER	These kids are walking around with big walls around them.
MOTHER	What did they take?
TEACHER	I wish I could figure out a way to get through —
MOTHER	What did they take from Jody?
TEACHER	Oh, I'm not sure. (*fishing out the poem*) This.

>   *It is in a pitiful state. The PARENTS fit it together.*

TEACHER   It's beside the point.

JODY   Not to me it isn't.

TEACHER   If I could get at their feelings somehow...

FATHER   Look.

>   *The PARENTS gather around the poem and read through it with increasing enjoyment.*

                    Somewhere a roaring giant roams
                    Nobody's safe in their homes

MOTHER   He towers and glowers

FATHER   And stomps through the flowers

TEACHER   This is good...
                    Watch out, Alan and Crystal and Mr. Beantree
                    /The monster is coming to eat you three...

JODY   The monster is coming to eat you three...

MOTHER   Sorry about that...

JODY   I'm not.

TEACHER   (*laughing*) ... he's getting grosser and grosser.

FATHER   Garbage can lid...

MOTHER   ...terrible scowling...

FATHER   Who is the giant who is so mad?...

JODY   (*sadly*) It's me.

MOTHER	The monster is me. (*anguished*) Oh... Jody...
TEACHER	This is awful.
FATHER	I thought it was pretty good.
TEACHER	Not the poem. Her poems are wonderful!
JODY	Wonderful?
TEACHER	So much feeling.

PARENTS look at each other, complimented.

FATHER	So what do you want us to do? Talk to her?
MOTHER	Take away her privileges?
JODY	No!
TEACHER	So much feeling. Maybe that's it! Sure, it's been staring at me all along! If it had teeth it would have jumped up and bit me!
FATHER	Pardon?
TEACHER	Yes!
MOTHER	Mr. Beantree?
TEACHER	Thank you so much for coming in. You've been very helpful.
MOTHER	We have?
TEACHER	(*waving a piece of JODY's poem*) And so has Jody. Oh, yes — what a great idea!
FATHER	If you say so.

JODY	So that was the meeting /with my parents —
FATHER	Anyway I'm sure /once she's had a chance...
MOTHER	Will you call us and let us know how things turn out?
TEACHER	Of course.

Exit everyone except JODY.

JODY	I hate these little meetings where the teacher and the parents discuss you. You never know what's going to happen next!
TEACHER	(*entering cheerfully*) Good morning, class.

The students assemble.

CLASS	Good morning, Mr. Beantree.
TEACHER	Now, yesterday we had a little trouble in the school yard, didn't we?
CLASS	Yes, Mr. Beantree.
TEACHER	And what do you think your punishment should be?
JODY	(*muttering*) Hang us by the neck until we are dead.
TEACHER	(*imitating the sheriff*) Hanging is too good fer the likes of you varmints.

The class does not know what to make of this.

(*normal voice*) No, I had something quite different in mind. Do you all know why you got so angry with one another yesterday?

They all start to talk at the same time.

JODY   Alan took/ my poem and Crystal grabbed it and they ripped it up and I don't care what they think — but I wanted to keep it — and I got really mad and that's what happened and it was a dirty rotten thing to do.

ALAN   It wasn't my fault. Crystal/ told me to do it and how was I supposed to know she'd run after me and she pushed me and I fell and scraped my knee and it really hurt and she called me stupid and then Crystal grabbed it and she tried to take it off her and then it ripped but I didn't rip it — she ripped it herself.

CRYSTAL   Who cares about her stinky little poem anyway and if she's so good why would she fight in the school yard and besides she kicked me and she got dirt over my nice jeans and she scratched my arm. See! And I'm going to have an ugly scar there for the rest of my life maybe and it's not fair /because she started it. She started it.

TEACHER   Stop. Stop. Alright. Now, tell me how you feel.

            Again they talk at the same time.

CRYSTAL   She's /rotten and I hate her...

ALAN   I /don't care how she feels...

JODY   I don't want to be their friend...

TEACHER   Wait, wait. That's how you feel about each other, right?

CLASS   Right.

TEACHER   Now tell me how you feel about yourself.

            Silence.

CRYSTAL   That's hard.

ALAN	How I feel?
JODY	About me?
TEACHER	Yes.
ALAN	How am I supposed to feel?
TEACHER	Just however you do feel.

Silence.

Who wants to go first.

CRYSTAL	Just stand up and say how we feel?
TEACHER	Why not?
CRYSTAL	It'd be —like — embarrassing.
JODY	Could we make up a poem about it?
TEACHER	(*secret triumph*) Poems? Alright, get out your pencils.
ALAN	Aw no.
TEACHER	What's wrong?
ALAN	I can't ever figure out how to make the words sound the same.
TEACHER	Don't worry about it. I told you poetry doesn't have to rhyme.
ALAN	Oh yeah.
TEACHER	Ready?

The children nod.

TEACHER	Get to work then.

The children don't write.

Come on. Put pen to paper.

JODY	(*despair*) Nothing's happening.
CRYSTAL	Mr. Beantree, would you give us an example?
TEACHER	Alright, alright. Let me see now. Uh ...

There once was a teacher named Beantree
Who wanted his students to write Poetry
His class was...

He breaks off and gets serious.

No, no. That won't work. You're right, Crystal. It is hard to say how we really feel. Let me try again.

(*writing on the board*) Teachers hide how they feel
And sometimes
It's the thing to do.
But not now.
So here's how I feel?
Scared.
Scared my lesson won't work
Scared we'll hurt each other
Scared we won't be friends
Scared we'll harden up
And squeeze up
And shut up.
I'm feeling scared.

Pause.

CRYSTAL	That's a poem?
TEACHER	Sort of.

ALAN   I can make up one like that.

TEACHER   Can you, Alan?

ALAN   Sure.

                Everybody is writing furiously.

TEACHER   Put your hands up when you —

                Everybody puts their hands up.

                Wonderful. Now who wants to go first.

                ALAN gets up, shyly.

TEACHER   Alan.

ALAN   I hate it when they call me stupid...

TEACHER   A little louder, Alan.

ALAN   I hate it when they call me stupid
                Because everything changes sizes
                Like everybody changes into big trees
                With branches.
                'Cept me.
                I get little —
                Like a bug.

                I hate it when they call me stupid
                Because everything changes speeds
                Like everybody blasts off
                'Till I can't see them anymore.
                I just get slower and slower
                And then I stop.

JODY   Do you really feel like that?

ALAN   Yeah.

JODY   Oh.

             Pause.

TEACHER   Thank you Alan. Very good.

ALAN   Really?

TEACHER   Really.

ALAN   (*surprised*) Oh!

TEACHER   Next?

JODY   Okay, this is how I've been feeling

             One day the words dried up
             I opened my mouth
             And out came guess what?
             Some sand came out
             And an old leaf
             And a pair of socks
             But no words.
             I took a big breath
             And out came a dried flower
             And some purple cough drops.
             I tried again
             I coughed
             And out came a nothing.
             Nothing came out
             Nothing.

             She opens her mouth and pauses.

             No lines
             No paper
             Not even a little white feather
             To write in the air

TEACHER   So you haven't been having much fun.

JODY	Nope.
TEACHER	I'm sorry. Next. (*pause*) Crystal.
CRYSTAL	My shoes are very nice And they cost a great big price—
TEACHER	Crystal?
CRYSTAL	Yes, Mr. Beantree?
TEACHER	This is not about your shoes, Crystal.
CRYSTAL	No sir.
TEACHER	It is about your soul.
CRYSTAL	Pardon?
ALAN	(*pointing to her desk*) She wrote something else.
CRYSTAL	Shut up.
TEACHER	Do you want to share, Crystal?
CRYSTAL	Not really.
TEACHER	Come on. If I can do it, you can do it.

   CRYSTAL picks up a second piece of paper.

Go ahead.

CRYSTAL   "What It's Like To Be Me" by Crystal Delisle.

                   It's scary to be me
                   Up on a shelf
                   All by myself
                   Looking down
                   At everybody else
                   Scared I'll fall
                   But scared I won't.
                   I don't
                   Want to be up here
                   My whole life
                   All by myself
                   On this stupid shelf.

She throws it down.

It's dumb.

JODY   No it isn't.

ALAN   No it isn't.

TEACHER   No it isn't.

CRYSTAL   Really?

TEACHER   So, how do you feel about each other now?

ALAN   Good.

CRYSTAL   Better.

JODY   Happy I think.

TEACHER   Good as a what, Alan?

ALAN   Good as a clam!

TEACHER   Crystal?

CRYSTAL	Better than a birthday party!
TEACHER	Jody?
JODY	Happy as a — a lizard.
TEACHER	Ahah.
ALAN	A flying lizard?
JODY	Yeah, exactly!
TEACHER	And that, class, is the power of poetry.

Bell rings.

ALAN	(*to CRYSTAL*) Want to play catch?
CRYSTAL	Sure.
ALAN	(*to JODY*) Well, don't just stand there.
CRYSTAL	Come on!
JODY	I'm coming!

The End.

Weird Kid

Playwright's Introduction

I wrote *Weird Kid* while resident playwright for The Globe Theatre in Regina, Saskatchewan. Brian Way, the famous British drama specialist, was going to direct but he fell ill and I fell director. I had always said that the playwright who directs his own plays has a fool for a director but there I was. Somebody gave me a hat that said director on the front and writer on the back. I didn't know whether I was coming or going.

What was great, though — and I think it was due to their acting talent rather than my directing ability — was the way the cast caught the natural speech rhythms of a group of young people. A writer and a company both succeed when the dialogue seems to hang so naturally on the lips.

The play was performed by actors who were graduates of theatre schools, older than the age of the characters they played. The classroom setting was suggested by wooden boxes arranged at first in formidable disarray and then tidied up into the semblance of a classroom. The audiences sat around the acting area in a circle. It toured Saskatchewan schools from September, 1988 to May, 1989.

Why did I write this play? I think somewhere in me my childhood still exists. There is a weird little Rex Deverell still trying to find acceptance — to fit in. But if I'm the weird kid I'm also the kid who was cruel to the weird kid. And I'm the mature kid who regrets it all and wonders how to take responsibility. So I wrote this play to explore all of that. Does it work for you too? Do you recognise yourself in my dilemma? Did we reach one another? I hope so because that's why I write.

Weird Kid was first produced by the Globe Theatre, Sept. 1988 at the Palliser Heights School, Moose Jaw, and toured schools through the 88/89 season, with the following cast:

Kelly Bricker	JENNIFER
Richard Clarkin	TIM
Stephen Fielden	BEN
Tannis Kowalchuk	TRISH

The characters in this play are students in the middle grades of school, ages 12 - 14.

Directed by Rex Deverell.
Designer - Jo Dibb.
Stage Manager - Leslie Kelly.

WEIRD KID

The suggestion of a school classroom in shambles.

VOICE (*amplified over a P.A. system*) Your attention please. The following students will report to the principal's office immediately: Tim Kowalchuck, Ben MacFarlane, Trish Klein and Jennifer Small. Tim Kowalchuck, Ben MacFarlane, Trish Klein and Jennifer Small please report to the principal's office immediately.

The students are lined up as if in the towering presence of a school principal.

TIM No, Sir, I didn't!

TRISH No!

BEN No, Sir.

JENNIFER I wouldn't do anything like that, honest!

TIM The first we knew about it was when we walked in this morning.

TRISH We were just as surprised as everybody else.

BEN Why would we want to wreck our own classroom?

TIM I know but —

JENNIFER We didn't even see each other over the weekend — except that Trish and me went to a movie Saturday afternoon. (*pause*) Trish and I.

TRISH   Why would we do that? I mean if we did it why would we leave our names on the board?

BEN   Yeah.

TIM   Right.

The invisible Mr. Phillips walks across his office and produces certain objects. The eyes of the students widen in surprise.

JENNIFER Yes, Mr. Phillips. That's my notebook.

TRISH   Yes, Mr. Phillips, that's my pencil case. I lost it a long time ago.

TIM   Yes, Mr. Phillips, that's my math text.

BEN   Yes, Sir. That's my library card.

TRISH   Where did you get all that?

TIM & JENNIFER Hall floor?

BEN   Mr. Phillips, if we had done it — and we didn't, honest — it would have been really stupid to drop our stuff all down the hall.

TRISH   Running? You think we were running? But we weren't even there.

TIM   We weren't. I don't know what else to say.

BEN   We didn't trash the room.

TRISH   Somebody else must've left those things there. Maybe they just wanted to make it look like we did it.

JENNIFER Yeah.

BEN	Right.
TRISH	I don't know why.
TIM	But it wasn't us.
TRISH	That's all we know. It wasn't us.

After a moment of listening they all groan.

TIM But there's nothing more we can — (*pause*) yes, Sir.

They stand aside as he leaves the office and then they follow along in a depressed procession back to the classroom.

TRISH But this isn't fair! It isn't! It isn't! Why the —

The others try to shut her up.

Why should we have to clean it up when we didn't wreck it in the first place? (*pause*) Yes, Sir.

The sound of a door slamming. They are jolted. It is like a sentence of death.

Dork brain.

TIM Don't make it worse.

TRISH Well he is. (*imitating the principal*) "Maybe you should just stay in here for a while, clean up the damage and think about things." Thanks a lot.

BEN "Come and see me when you have reconsidered your position."

JENNIFER He isn't ever going to believe us.

TIM Probably not.

TRISH	I'm not gonna apologize for something I didn't do. He can leave me here until I'm a toothless old lady before I'll do that.
JENNIFER	Speak for yourself. I want to get out of here.
BEN	(*mock hysterics*) I've gotta get outa here! I've gotta get out, I tell you!
JENNIFER	Ben.
BEN	I can't take it. I've got claustrophobia — I'm going to break. I'll tell them anything they want. I'm going berserk in here! The walls are closing in. To be locked up in classroom forever. A fate worse than death. Arrrggh!
TIM	Unless they expel us.

This sobers everyone up.

BEN	I didn't think of that.

Pause.

JENNIFER	(*clearly distressed*) What'll we do?
TIM	It's okay, Jen. We'll come up with something, eh?
BEN	Sure we will.
TRISH	We'd better.
JENNIFER	Like what?
TIM	Well — like —
BEN	Like —

TRISH	Like —

There is a long pause.

JENNIFER	Well?
BEN	If we could only think of who did it.
TIM	(*after a moment*) It really wasn't any of you guys, was it?

Everybody protests at the same time.

TRISH	Oh, come on!
BEN	Are you kidding?
JENNIFER	You know us better than that.
TIM	I didn't really think so. (*pause*) Can you prove it?
TRISH	Can you?
TIM	I was away over the weekend with my parents.
BEN	When did you get back?
TIM	Last night.
BEN	Maybe that's when it happened. It could have happened anytime over the last forty-eight hours. You could have done it.
TIM	(*conceding*) Yeah.
BEN	I could have. Any of us could have.
OTHERS	But we didn't.

BEN | Of course not but — (*surveying the wreckage*) somebody sure did and, Ladies and Gentlemen of the Jury...

OTHERS | Ben.

BEN | I can't help it. This calls for a great criminal lawyer and I'm it. So — I ask you, Ladies and Gentlemen of the Jury, since none of us committed this heinous crime, who in fact did?

TIM | That's the question alright.

BEN | Think.

TIM | I'm thinking — I'm thinking.

TRISH | I'm too mad to think.

BEN | Think!

JENNIFER | I don't know. There's no way we can know. It could have been anybody.

TRISH | No, not just anybody. (*after a moment*) Somebody who wanted to get us real bad.

BEN | Now you're thinking.

JENNIFER | Oh, come off it.

TRISH | Why else would they leave our names on the board and our stuff all around the place?

TIM | A frame up?

TRISH | Of course.

JENNIFER | Who'd want to do that? We're nice.

BEN	Right. We're the most popular kids in the school. Least I am.
TIM	You're the most popular jerk in the school.
BEN	Speak for yourself.
JENNIFER	You'd have to be weird to hate anybody that much.
TIM	I think we're dealing with somebody pretty weird here.
TRISH	That's it. Think — who might be psycho enough to do stuff like this.
JENNIFER	Out of the whole school?
TRISH	No.
TIM	Probably just out of our class, right?
BEN	Probably.
TRISH	Exactly. Somebody in our class who knows us. The one person who is just weird enough to do something this strange. There's only one person who would do something like this.
	Pause. Realisation dawns on the others almost simultaneously.
JENNIFER	Babs?
BEN	Babs.
TIM	Babs.
TRISH	Babs Story.
BEN	That's it — it couldn't have been anyone else.

JENNIFER	She'd have to be the one.
TIM	Makes sense.
BEN	(*heading for the door*) Let's go tell Mr. Phillips.
JENNIFER	Yeah.

JENNIFER and TRISH follow him.

TIM	Hold it, hold it!
BEN & JENNIFER	What?
TIM	Let's think about this. We don't have any proof. All we've got is our suspicions.
TRISH	Well, we can — (*pause*) He's right.
JENNIFER	But it's all we've got. Better than nothing.
BEN	Least it'll take the heat off us.
TIM	Okay — I'm old Phillips — (*setting up a scene*) and you come in — Yes, MacFarlane? You're ready to confess?
BEN	(*falling into line*) Yes, Sir — I mean no, Sir. We've just figured out who — er —
TIM	(*ominous*) Vandalized?
BEN	Our classroom. It was Babs Story.
TIM	Yes?
BEN	That's all. It wasn't us. It was Babs Story.
TIM	Are you sure?

BEN	Yes. (*pause*) Sort of.
TIM	Be careful, young man.
BEN	Pardon?
TIM	This is a serious accusation. You are already in very deep trouble. Don't add to your list of crimes. Now why do you believe Babs Story is the vandal.
BEN	She's the only one wacko enough to do it.
TIM	I beg your pardon?
BEN	(*hesitating*) There's nobody else in our class who's that — that — wacko.
TIM	In your opinion.
BEN	Ask anybody.
TIM	That is not good enough.
TRISH	And he thinks we left our things at the scene of the crime.
TIM	And you left your things at the scene of the crime. All of the evidence points to you.
JENNIFER	(*bursting in*) She was out to get us.
TIM	Why?

Pause.

BEN	I don't know.
JENNIFER	Well — like she acts like she's mad all the time — and —

TIM	Yes?
JENNIFER	— and she's not like normal.
TIM	Yes?
JENNIFER	For instance she's kind of dozey a lot —
TIM	Yes?
JENNIFER	And sometimes she's — (*lamely*) kinda smelly.
TIM	(*exploding*) This is despicable! You children have been picking on this girl ever since she came to this school last fall.
JENNIFER	We have not.
TIM	I think you have. I'm ashamed of you. Ashamed! Have you anything else to say for yourselves or shall I call your parents down here? (*pause*) Well?
BEN	(*slumping*) I see what you mean. We're sunk. We don't have anything.
JENNIFER	We haven't been picking on her ever since she came to school.
TRISH	Yes we have. Think about it.
JENNIFER	Not me.
BEN	Not me — well, maybe a little.
TIM	Maybe a lot.
BEN	Come on — she brought it on herself. Remember that first day — when she first came into the class? (*doing a somewhat unpleasant caricature*) So what's it to ya — I couldn't care less if it's your book. Gimme that

	— how'm I suppose to do my homework if I don't have a book — you're a bunch of jerk faces — you guys — I'm gonna be a movie star when I grow up. I was already in two movies where I useta live...
TRISH	(*aside to JENNIFER*) Yeah, "The Bride of Frankenstein" and "Return of The Blob".
	They both laugh.
BEN	(*as Babs*) I heard that.
TRISH	See?
JENNIFER	What?
TRISH	You did pick on her.
JENNIFER	All I did was...
TIM	Laugh, right?
JENNIFER	(*weakly*) Laugh. At Trish's stupid joke.
BEN	We all laughed. (*to TIM*) You too.
TIM	I guess I did.
TRISH	I thought I was kinda witty.
JENNIFER	We tried to make friends — I did, anyway.
BEN	Yeah, we weren't really cruel or anything.
JENNIFER	I remember the first day she was there I walked right up to her and I said, "Wanna eat lunch with me?"
TRISH	Yeah and she said — "Forget it — I don't want to eat lunch with you."

TIM	No — she said — she said — I can't remember — wasn't it like — I can't today. I gotta go home.
JENNIFER	And I said "Don't you have your lunch?"
TIM	I forgot it. Why don't you just leave me alone?
JENNIFER	I was just trying to be nice.
TIM	Well forget it — You don't have to be nice to me. And (*with Trish*) what makes you think I'd want to eat lunch with you anyway?
TRISH	... (*with TIM*) what makes you think I'd want to eat lunch with you anyway?
JENNIFER	There, see?
BEN	So what's your point?
TIM	That this is complicated — more complicated than you—
TRISH	It's not complicated at all — Babs Story is just a spoilt brat—
TIM	Sure she's gross and everything. But if we really want to show that she's the one who did all this we have to sort it all out — get all the facts straight. Then we can go to Mr. Phillips with the whole story.
BEN	Like what she's done to us up to now.
TIM	Yeah — or even what we've done to her. Then he might believe us.
JENNIFER	Brilliant.
TRISH	I coulda thought of that.
BEN	Oh yeah?

TIM	All we have to do is remember every time any of us had anything to do with her.
TRISH	(*dismayed*) Oh boy.
JENNIFER	Where do we start?
TIM	Anywhere, I guess. Whatever we remember.
BEN	Okay, let's start with this. (*resuming his role as a criminal lawyer*) Mr. Phillips, Your Honour — Your Dishonour, Your Fatheadedness —
OTHERS	Ben!
BEN	Whatever — Ladies and Gentlemen of the Jury — I intend beyond a shadow of a doubt to expose the defendant, Babs Story, for the criminal she is. I call as my first witness, Patricia Klein. (*to TRISH*) Do you swear to tell the truth, the whole truth and nothing but the truth, so help you God?
TRISH	This is serious, Ben.
BEN	I'm serious. What were you doing on or about...the lunch room about a month ago?
TRISH	Eating lunch?
TIM	Give the lady a cigar.
BEN	This day in particular, there was only one place left and you had to sit beside someone you didn't particularly want to sit beside —
TRISH	(*remembering*) Oh yeah.
JENNIFER	(*remembering*) Right.
BEN	Who was that person?

TRISH	Babs.
BEN	Exactly. (*arranging the stage*) Now, your Honour, with the court's permission I'd like to arrange a little demonstration here. (*he has pulled chairs up to a table or desk*) Jennifer — you play the part of the defendant, Babs Story.
JENNIFER	But I wasn't there— I just heard about it after.
BEN	You are eating your lunch —
TIM	This time you have a lunch.

She pretends to be eating.

BEN	Yes, this time she has a lunch. And Trish comes in. She sits down beside her. Observe, Your Honour...

TRISH squeezes in beside Babs and they look to BEN for more direction.

Did she say anything?

TRISH	Yeah, I think so —
JENNIFER	Hi.
TRISH	I couldn't find any place else —
JENNIFER	What do I do now?
TRISH	(*pause*) And then you just get up and throw my lunch on the floor and say I hate you, I hate you.
JENNIFER	(*giggling as she does it*) I hate you, I hate you.
BEN	M'Lord, the Crown rests its case.
TIM	Wait a minute. Are you sure that's what happened?

BEN	Precisely. I saw it myself.
TIM	(*to the girls*) Would you do it again?
TRISH	Come on, Tim. That's what happened.
TIM	It's like something's been left out.
TRISH	Well, I can't remember every itty bitty detail — but that's more or less what —
TIM	She wouldn't get that upset over nothing —
BEN	That's what she's like —
TIM	You guys, do it right, okay? I mean nothing is going to come out of this unless we remember all the details. It's the only way Phillips is going to believe us. It's the only way he'll know we aren't just giving our version of it — if we've worked it all out. Now there's gotta be more to it than that, isn't there, Trish?
TRISH	Maybe a little.
TIM	Okay, you were here. Babs was sitting there. You sat down. What did she do right when you sat down?
TRISH	She just kept eating, I guess —
JENNIFER	Like what?
TRISH	Like something kinda smelly —
TIM	You said something, didn't you?
BEN	Your Worship, my friend is badgering the witness.
TIM	(*to BEN*) Buzz off.
BEN	(*protesting*) Your Worship!

TIM   (*showing him a fist*) Ben.

                BEN is quiet.

                Okay.

TRISH   (*a certain amount of disdain*) What's that?

JENNIFER   A sandwich.

TRISH   I know that, stu- (*catching herself*) What's in it?

JENNIFER   Onions and garlic sausage.

BEN   And, Mr. Judge, Sir — sitting at close quarters with this — this person who is eating onions and garlic sausage, Patricia didn't even wrinkle her nose —

TRISH   Well, maybe I did a little... I don't know what she was eating — but it stunk. I mean what would you do if you were sitting beside this slob and she was eating yuck.

BEN   (*annoyed*) You're not helping our case.

TIM   The absolute truth, Ben. It's the only thing that'll save us.

TRISH   Okay, okay. We'll do it right. This is my lunch. (*miming*)

JENNIFER   This is my lunch.

                Once more TRISH sits down. This time they try to play it as it happened.

JENNIFER   Hi.

TRISH   Hello.

They eat away at their lunches for a time. JENNIFER becomes aware that TRISH is watching her.

TRISH (*nasty*) What's that?

JENNIFER A sandwich.

TRISH I know that, stupid. What's in it?

JENNIFER Onions and garlic sausage.

TRISH makes a face.

JENNIFER You didn't have to sit here, you know.

TRISH I didn't have any choice.

They eat in silence. The tension is growing between them.

JENNIFER Keep your garbage on your own side of the table, okay?

TRISH I didn't do anything. You're the one eating garbage.

JENNIFER explodes and throws over the desk they were using as a table.

JENNIFER I hate you! I hate you!

TIM Hey, take it easy.

BEN Are you alright?

JENNIFER Yeah, I'm okay.

TRISH You sure?

JENNIFER	Yeah. It got kinda real there.
TRISH	(*with the others*) Yeah, it did. (*to the others*) Anyway there, you see? That's exactly what happened!
JENNIFER	Well, you see why, doncha?
TRISH	She is just basically a nasty person.
JENNIFER	What was the girl supposed to do?
TRISH	She doesn't like me and I don't like her.
BEN	Your Honour — in this situation there wasn't any need for this kind of violent behaviour. You can see now what sort of a person we are dealing with here—
TRISH	The sort of person who'd wreck a classroom just to get back at us...
TIM	The person who might have some reason to get back at us.
BEN	I guess we might have been mean to her sometimes...
TIM	So that was one situation. Okay. Who remembers another one.
BEN	The video project.
JENNIFER	What did Babs have to do with that?
TIM	She was in our group.
TRISH	No she wasn't. We didn't choose her...
BEN	She came in late. (*to TRISH*) You be Babs.
TRISH	No way.

BEN	Why not.
TRISH	I don't want to be her.
TIM	Somebody's gotta be.
TRISH	We don't have to act it out — we can just try to remember what happened.
JENNIFER	No — this is good. You find out a lot this way.
TRISH	Like what?
JENNIFER	Believe me.
TIM	Let's just try it, okay?
TRISH	You do it then.

Everybody laughs.

TIM	Alright. I'll be Babs.
TRISH	No. That'd be just silly.
TIM	Silly? Just watch. Remember what we were doing? We were just getting our idea together about rock videos — and how that'd be what we'd do for the class, right? And —
BEN	(*to TRISH*) You were up on the desk and we were all making like .... (*he names a popular rock group*).
JENNIFER	Right. We were doing .... (a current hit).

They all get into recreating the song. In the first production we used "Fat", the Weird Al satire of Michael Jackson's "Bad".

TRISH   (*at the peak of the fun*) And then Babs came in.

TIM   Right. Babs came in.

> *His version of Babs is not an impersonation so much as how he could act if he were in Babs' situation. When the others play Babs later they fall into this style of role playing. Tim as Babs is standing at the entrance way watching the others carry on.*

TIM   What are you doing?

> *They don't hear.*

                 (*louder*) I said, what are you doing?

BEN   A rock video. What's it look like?

TIM   Stupid.

TRISH   What are you doing here?

TIM   Mrs. Graham.

JENNIFER   You're supposed to be in group 5.

TIM   There were too many in group 5. Mrs. Graham told me to come here.

BEN   But we've already started.

TIM   Why are you doing a rock video? I thought we were supposed to do something about — like — what makes our lives different from — like other peoples' lives—

JENNIFER   Like that's what we're doing, aren't we?

BEN   What is the big symbol of our generation?

TIM	A moving van.
TRISH	Rock videos.
JENNIFER	Come on. You can be the drummer.
TIM	I don't want to be no drummer.
BEN	Any drummer.
TIM	Shut up. All I know is we're supposed to be making up something about our lives today.
BEN	I just said that's what we are doing. Rock videos. Come on. We don't have a lot of time. Are you going to join in or not?
TIM	What if I got a different idea?
TRISH	We don't have enou —
JENNIFER	Well, we should listen —
TIM	You won't want to do it —
BEN	Sure, if it's better than our idea — (*to the others*) Right?
JENNIFER	Sure.
TRISH	We're wasting time. What's your idea?
TIM	I said a moving van.
TRISH	I don't get it.
TIM	I think a lot of people — like families — like — move around the country a lot more than they useta.

BEN   (*to the others*) Do you want to do 'moving around the country' instead of rock videos?

           The reply is silence.

           That's what I thought. (*to TIM/Babs*) See? Okay, let's get on with it.

           They start back into the song.

TIM   (*interrupting*) Could you do the rock video about moving?

BEN   No.

TIM   Why not?

TRISH   There's no song like that —

TIM   There could be. We could —

JENNIFER   Either help or keep quiet, alright? (*pause*) Well, we didn't have any time, did we?

TRISH   She just wanted her own way.

TIM   She wrote the song, you know.

           The others do not know how to respond.

TRISH   Babs?

TIM   (*fishing in his school bag and mumbling*) I don't have any place to go... But I'm just movin' on... Something, something...

BEN   It's a song?

TIM   Yeah... (*consulting a piece of paper*) They told me it'd be good here...

TRISH	How does it go?
TIM	(*trying to remember the tune*) Just a minute... (*with growing confidence he begins to sing*)

> I don't have any place to go
> but I'm just movin' on
>
> They told me it'd be good here
> maybe
> Dad and Mom might get along here
> Dad might even get a job here
> maybe
>
> Now we're movin' on from here
> Don't have any better place to go
>
> No place worse though,
> Movin' on.
>
> Don't know where to go
> but I'm goin'.

BEN	Babs wrote that?
JENNIFER	How did you learn it?
TIM	A cassette. She gave me a cassette a couple weeks after the video project. I guess she wanted to show us.
BEN	We might've gotten a better mark with that.
TRISH	When you get an F minus, any direction is up. Geeze, Babs Story. Who woulda thought.
BEN	Did she move a lot?
JENNIFER	Kinda obvious, eh?

TIM: I asked around. They say her family isn't too together — her Dad doesn't show up much.

TRISH: We all have problems. That's no excuse.

BEN: Well, your Honour — we admit that we looked down on the defendant. We admit we misjudged her. In fact it's getting to look more and more like she's the only one who had enough reasons to want to get us into deep — er — difficulty, Sir.

TRISH: That's right.

TIM: Okay. What else have we got? Jen — what about the time —

JENNIFER: Isn't this enough? (*starting for the door*) Hey, Ben, that sounds good, eh? Let's go.

TIM: What's your hurry?

JENNIFER: Let's get it over with.

TIM: What about the time you were best friends with her.

JENNIFER: It didn't last very long.

BEN: Yeah — what was that about, anyway?

JENNIFER: Nothing.

TIM: Well, tell us then.

JENNIFER: It's my business.

TRISH: What is?

JENNIFER: It's not something I'm proud of, okay?

Pause.

JENNIFER	Alright, you know how last year I was new at this school — and it took a long time to make friends with anybody and finally you guys got to be my friends. Well for a while this year Trish started to act kinda strange —
TRISH	I did not!
JENNIFER	I mean you were going to movies and stuff with Ben and Tim — and you wouldn't call me up or anything and see if I might want to go, you know what I mean?
TRISH	(*surprised*) Really?
JENNIFER	Yes, really. So I kinda made up with Babs.
TRISH	What a choice.
JENNIFER	To get back at you.
TRISH	Oh. But I didn't do that on purpose —
JENNIFER	I know that now—
TRISH	Oh, Jen...
JENNIFER	Oh, Trish...

The boys are about to vomit.

TIM	I hate to break in on this intimate scene — but we're talking about Babs.
JENNIFER	Yeah, Babs. Well, she just got caught in the middle. I guess the worse part of it was when I made arrangements to go shopping with her.
TRISH	The day I ran into you at Market Square Mall?

JENNIFER   I kinda planned that too. I knew you'd probably show up. (*to BEN*) You be Babs this time.

BEN   Yucky girls' stuff. Let Trish do it. She hasn't done it yet —

JENNIFER   No, Trish is in this.

BEN   (*resigned*) What do I do?

JENNIFER   Well, it took me a while to persuade her to come. She said she didn't want to buy anything and she didn't have the money to take the bus downtown — and I said come on anyway because I'd gotten a lot of money for my birthday from my grandmother and I still need to buy a pair of jeans or something and (*to BEN*) you have such great taste...

TRISH   Oh-boy.

JENNIFER   Right. Anyway that's what I told her and (*to BEN*) you fall for it and my mom gives us a ride and drops us off ... but you still don't have any money... What are you going to get, Babs?

BEN   (*playing the part realistically*) I told you I couldn't buy anything.

JENNIFER   (*keeping an eye out for TRISH*) I know — but I thought you probably could buy some little thing.

BEN   Well, I can't. Let's go and get your — boy, look at that.

JENNIFER   What?

BEN   That dirt bike — no, she wouldn't be interested in a dirt bike —

JENNIFER	It was one of those keyboard things — electronic piano or something. How did you know she stopped like that?
BEN	If she's like me — whenever I don't have any money I always see something really expensive I'd really like. That really bugs me.
JENNIFER	She looked at it like she'd never be able to buy it — not in a thousand years.
BEN	(*as Babs*) Those keyboards — you can make any sound you could ever want. You don't even have to write it down or anything. You just play it and it plays back what ever you think up.
JENNIFER	It's probably not that easy, Babs. Let's start with Chez Lean Jeans — and if they don't have anything maybe Jiffy Sports and then I'll try Eatons and maybe Zellers, okay? Hey, look at those...
BEN	They're nice...
JENNIFER	No — they're too ordinary...
BEN	Are you sure you want me to help?
JENNIFER	I wouldn't have asked you, would I?
BEN	I guess not...
JENNIFER	(*suddenly*) There's Trish Klein. (*waving*) Hi, Trish.
TRISH	(*coming over*) Hi, Jenny. Fancy meeting you.
JENNIFER	Say hello to my very good friend Babs.
TRISH	Hello, Babs.
BEN	Hullo.

TRISH   So what are you doing?

JENNIFER   Buying some jeans. Babs is helping me, aren't you, Babs?

BEN   I guess so.

TRISH   How come I haven't heard from you?

JENNIFER   How come I haven't heard from you?

TRISH   I thought you'd call.

JENNIFER   I thought *you'd* call.

                Pause.

TRISH   Are you going to the party tonight?

JENNIFER   What party?

TRISH   Ben and Tim are cooking something up. They said they were inviting you.

JENNIFER   I don't know...

TRISH   You can come. Hey, I'll stop on the way and we can walk over together, okay?

JENNIFER   I'll think about it. I'll probably come. Yeah, I'll come. What time?

TRISH   Eight.

JENNIFER   Great!

TRISH   What sort of jeans are you going to buy?

JENNIFER   I don't know. Got any ideas?

TRISH	To tell you the truth there's this new brand over at the Slack Shack? I've been thinking about — you know — at least trying on a pair. Wanna go over there?
JENNIFER	Sure! (*to Babs as an after thought*) Coming?
BEN	No, it's alright. Go ahead.
JENNIFER	(*breaking out of the scene*) That's exactly the way she sounded. You could have been there. How did you know?
BEN	I sorta guessed.
TIM	There's a picture coming clear.
BEN	And so, your Honour, Sir, perhaps you can see a history of meanness, a building up of hurt and little insults, a powder keg, as they say, just waiting to explode.
JENNIFER	Yeah.
TRISH	Still, didn't give her any right to —
BEN	And then there was the great tease episode. I started that myself.
JENNIFER	Oh, no. I hate this, Ben. It makes us sound so awful.
BEN	Truth, Jen. It's the only thing that'll save us. Right, Tim?
TIM	Go ahead.
BEN	(*going up to TRISH*) Hey, Babs!
TRISH	Go 'way.
BEN	Babs!

TRISH	I don't want to.
BEN	Babs.
TRISH	No, Ben.
BEN	Know what I heard, Babs?
TRISH	Ben, go away.
BEN	Somebody likes you.
TRISH	Not interested. (*but she falls into the role in spite of herself*)
BEN	Okay, I'll tell him you're not interested.
TRISH	Who?
BEN	Guess.
TRISH	I can't guess.
BEN	He told me not to tell you. But I'll tell you his initials.
TRISH	(*softly*) Okay.
BEN	Pardon?
TRISH	Okay.
BEN	Okay what?
TRISH	Tell me his initials.
BEN	Who's initials?
TRISH	Whoever — likes me.

BEN	T. K.
TIM	Oh no.
BEN	(*aside*) Sorry, Tim.
TRISH	Tim likes me?
JENNIFER	He told me, too. He's told everybody in the school. Tim Kowalchuck likes Babs Story.
TRISH	Everybody knows?
JENNIFER	Everybody knows.
BEN	Everybody in the school.
TRISH	And everybody is laughing.
BEN	I wouldn't say everybody.
JENNIFER	Not everybody. Look, there he is.
BEN	Tell him to come over here.
TRISH	No.
BEN	Go on. It won't hurt you.
JENNIFER	Go on.
TRISH	Tim?
TIM	What?
BEN	(*too loudly*) Come over here, Tim. Babs wants to ask you something.
TIM	(*coming closer*) What?

JENNIFER	Ask him for a date, Babs.

> *BEN and JENNIFER burst into laughter.*

TIM	What is this?
TRISH	Did you tell Ben that you liked me?
TIM	No way. Why?
TRISH	(*seeing that it is all fictitious*) Oh, nothing.

> *More laughter.*

TIM	(*walking away in disgust*) Give up, you guys.
TRISH	This isn't funny.
BEN	Babs didn't say that.
TRISH	She said it to herself.
TIM	Yeah, she must've...
TRISH	Why did you do that, Ben?
BEN	I was just having fun. You're the one to talk.
TRISH	This is different.
BEN	Why?
JENNIFER	Because you were being Babs this time?
TRISH	Yeah. (*pause*) And what if she liked Tim a little? Lots of people do.
TIM	Of course.
BEN	Especially if they are weird.

TRISH	Don't let it go to your head but people think you're nice.
JENNIFER	I don't think any of us are so nice.
TIM	Agreed. Not now.
BEN	I'll dispute that. (*the others glare at him*) Lighten up, everybody. I just wanted to have a little fun. (*pause*) Okay, you're right. It wasn't the most terrific — but okay, so look... (*to TRISH*) You're a girl —
TIM	Observant.
BEN	Shut up. (*to TRISH*) Trish, if we'd done that to you instead of Babs, what would you have done?
TRISH	Me? I would have gotten mad, for sure. I would have told you all off and then I might have laughed but inside I'd still be really hurt.
BEN	Right. But you wouldn't have gone and tried to tear the school down.
TIM	But if you were Babs?
TRISH	If I were Babs? Well, I guess I'd've gone home and cried a lot and then I might have remembered all the other times stuff was done to me — and I'd probably not be thinking too clearly, and I might decide to take it out on the school — just anything to hurt back for a change — instead of taking it all the time and then I might have thought about the four of us and written our names on the board and taken a few things of ours and thrown them around just to make it look like we had done it — because I might have been trying to say that we were responsible — and I guess maybe we were.
BEN	So, there you are, Your Honour. I rest my case.

JENNIFER	Pretty convincing.
TIM	Right. She was an unhappy person and we made her —
TRISH	Unhappier.

Pause.

BEN	Can we go to Phillips with all this?
TIM	If we tell it like we told ourselves.

The intercom beeps.

VOICE	Room 4?
TIM	Yes, Sir?
VOICE	Have you cleaned up in there?
JENNIFER	Yes, Sir.
BEN	More or less.
VOICE	I beg your pardon?
TRISH	Yes, Sir.
TIM	We've thought things over — I think we know what happened.
VOICE	Very well, come to the office.

Intercom clicks off.

JENNIFER	Let's go.
BEN	Yeah, let's go.

But none of them want to move.

TRISH	(*after a time*) Maybe we should tell him we did it?
JENNIFER	Are you crazy?
TRISH	It's just an idea.
TIM	What would it accomplish?
TRISH	Nothing, I guess. (*pause*) No. For one thing it might give us a chance to make it up to Babs — maybe we could help her somehow.
BEN	(*getting up*) She did it. She should take the consequences. Let's go.
TIM	Help her?
BEN	Nothing's going to help Babs.
JENNIFER	Nothing we could do.
TRISH	Nothing easy. (*pause*) I can't believe it's me saying this.
BEN	Me neither.
TIM	I like it.
BEN	(*in pain*) Tim.
TIM	We'd all have to stick together on it.
JENNIFER	But it would be lying.
BEN	Right. No way, man. I'm telling it like it happened.
TRISH	But we don't know that's what happened. Not for sure.

BEN	Oh yes we do. Yes we do. We know that is exactly what happened. We tell it any different and we get punished for what she did —
TRISH	That's the idea.
JENNIFER	Trish!
BEN	It doesn't make any sense.
TIM	You don't think it makes sense for us to take her punishment.
BEN	Of course not.
TIM	You sure?

This brings BEN up short. There is a long pause.

JENNIFER	Suppose we do. She won't thank us.
TRISH	Probably not.
BEN	It'd probably be the first time anybody ever did anything for her. (*pause*) Trish...
TRISH	What?
BEN	This is the most ridiculous thing I ever heard.
TRISH	I know. I must be going weird. Let's do it, okay?
JENNIFER	I'm scared.
TIM	Me too.
BEN	Are we going to do it or not?

Intercom beeps.

VOICE	Room 4?
EVERYONE	Coming.

They leave the room and their voices are heard echoing down the hallway.

The End.

In the first production, an actor would step forward after the curtain call.

ACTOR Thanks lot. We have some time left and we would like to hear what you think is going to happen in the principal's office once the students get there. Please turn to your neighbours and talk about it for a few seconds.

After an certain amount of discussion the actor may ask for reports from the groups or the cast may circulate among the audience and hear what they have to say. At the end of the time, it would be good to have a brief summary of the range of possibilities that have been talked about.

ACTOR Thank you for your comments. Most of us have probably felt like Babs Story from time to time — and we've probably been like the other kids, too. Maybe the next time we can make it different.

Video Wars

Sorry. War is Hell. Care to try again?

Playwright's Introduction

In 1990 I resigned my job at The Globe Theatre and I moved East to Toronto. It took me a long time to admit to anybody that I actually lived in Toronto. (That proves I'd really become a Westerner.) Bruce Griffin looked me up and asked if The Golden Horseshoe Players might do one of my plays, and later I wrote *Video Wars* for this company. The Gulf War was happening and I found myself watching it on CNN. Gosh it was exciting...just like science fiction, just like a video game, just like... Hey, wait a minute! Those are real people getting crushed and blasted apart.

I started to think about war refugess all over the world — Eastern Europe, Africa, Asia. Just up the street from us was a corner store and across the street was a school and kids went to the store every chance they had. Behind the counter was an Asian lady — beautiful in a way but old before her time. None of the kids knew anything about her — except that she counted their pennies and gave them popsicles. Could that be a setting for a play — a play that says "Hey, wait a minute!"

Video Wars had its first performance October 3, 1991 at Humber Summit Middle School, North York Board of Education, Ontario. It was directed by the talented actor/director, Richard Greenblatt who found a way of creating a war video game using the hands and the bodies of the actors in a cross between a puppet show and a dance. The actors were:

Donald Car

Heidimarie Guggi

David Matheson

Sam Rosenthal

Designer - Teresa Przybylski.
Stage Manager - Pamela Craig.

CHARACTERS

Four actors who can take on various roles

They are identified in the script by the names of their through characters NICK, KIM, BILLIE, and DARIN.

NICK
: a boy, about thirteen years old. The play is basically his own story and he will act as narrator as well as a character within it. He has the carefree, exuberant attitude of a child whose life has been without any great pain.

KIM
: a boy, perhaps twelve years old. He and his mother are recent refugees from a war-torn country. His mother is running the Handy Dandy Corner Store and he is often taken out of school to help make ends meet. I've left his nationality ambiguous. He is bright, has learned English fluently — picked up on the slang of his classmates but both his experiences and the need to mind the shop have set him apart from others his age. Although a composite, his story is based on true life accounts.

BILLIE
: A classmate of Nick, she is a girl who has made the choice to identify with the guys, pugnacious, competitive and determined.

DARIN
: another member of Nick's set. He is less secure than the others and often feels the need to prove himself. Nevertheless he provides a kind of audience for Nick and Billie.

Note about casting: with minor changes to the gender references in the text, the part of Kim may also be played by a girl. The first casting of the play was successfully "non traditional" in that the actor playing Kim was not a member of a visible minority and the actor playing Darin was.

Although written for four actors, the cast can be expanded to as many as sixteen.

VIDEO WARS

The interior of The Handy Corner Store, a small neighbourhood variety shop. The owners have recently installed an electronic video game to see if it will improve business. The store is near a school and from time to time the sounds of the school yard can be heard through the walls of the store. NICK enters wearing the latest cocky flamboyant style. He addresses the audience.

NICK Hi. I want to tell you about something that happened to me — oh, my name's Nick — anyway, something kinda important that happened to me one afternoon. I'll set the scene for you. This is THE HANDY DANDY CORNER GROCERY STORE — "The Handy" for short.

In the distance there is the sound of a school bell and children pouring into the playground.

That's the school I go to — right across the road. Me and my friends come in here all the time. You know — before school, bubble gum; at noon, Orange Sloshy Slurpies and stuff; after school, Chocolate Barfies and Bitter Sour Lemon twists — if we've got any money left. Kids come in here in like waves. First the little kids.

Suddenly the stage seems full of youngsters running around the store. They come up to the counter and address an unseen storekeeper.

DARIN I want a cream soda!

BILLIE	I want a Sloshy Slurpy. A little one. No, a big one. One with Smarties in it.
KIM	I want a red licorice. Is this enough money?
DARIN	(*to NICK*) Gimme a dime, okay? Okay? Gimme a dime! That's all I need to get some pop, okay? Gimme a dime.
BILLIE	Don't put those kind of Smarties. I just want the red ones. I said the red ones. I don't want those green kind. Take them out! Take them out! Yechhh!
KIM	How many can I have for this much money?
DARIN	Just give me a nickel, okay? Please? Pretty please. Aw, c'mon! One little nickel?
NICK	Out!

They vanish and the stage is quiet again.

NICK	Those were the little kids. Then a bunch of Senior High kids come in...

The actors return as teenagers — the unimpressionable age.

KIM	I'm cool.
BILLIE	I'm cool.
DARIN	I'm very cool.
KIM	A tube of Clearasil, please.
DARIN	What are you doing tonight?

BILLIE	I don't know. Maybe I'll call Stephie — unless Allison calls me in which case I'll call you but I probably won't because Dan called yesterday and he said that Laurie and Melanie were over and — you know. Or maybe I'll wash my hair. What are you doing tonight?
KIM	I don't know. Nothing, I guess — life is so boring.
DARIN	Yeah, boring.
BILLIE	Yeah. Call me, okay?
KIM	Okay.
BILLIE	Okay?
DARIN	Okay.
BILLIE	Okay.

The teenagers begin to leave.

KIM	Am I getting a zit right here? Do you see a zit?

Exit.

NICK	Those were the big kids. (*calling after them*) Get a life why doncha? (*to the audience*) And after that we take over — me and kids in my class.

DARIN and BILLIE return in their roles as NICK's classmates, sauntering through the store like gangsters — clearly in charge.

DARIN	Yo, Nick!
NICK	Yo, Darin! (*to audience*) That's Darin.
DARIN	Say what, Dude!

NICK   What!

                   They break up.

BILLIE   Yo, Guys.

NICK &
DARIN   Yo, Billie!

NICK   (*to audience*) This is Billie.

BILLIE   Give me five!

NICK &
DARIN   Five!

NICK   (*aside to audience*) Us. The only kids that matter.

DARIN and BILLIE strike poses with NICK. The three of them make up a formidable trio. BILLIE and NICK have a competitive edge to them and sometimes they compete with each other for 'territorial rights'. BILLIE is bright and alert. DARIN is the follower of the group and somewhat more timid — although he is always trying to find a way of asserting himself or gaining the others' approval. These three insult one another all the time, but they are usually good-natured about it.

NICK   It's noon hour and at noon hour we own this place.

KIM   (*entering*) I beg your pardon?

Although KIM is about the same age as the others, one knows he is not one of the set. His clothes are tidy and serviceable but not quite in style. He doesn't have an accent — and yet there is the odd word misplaced and the sense that English

	is not his mother tongue. He seems a little mature for his age — responsible.
NICK	(*to audience*) And this is Kim.
KIM	Who owns this place?
NICK	(*to audience*) His mother actually owns this place.
BILLIE	No, we do.
DARIN	Yeah, we do.
KIM	Excuse me?
BILLIE	This is our territory — like our turf, understand? We like dominate it.
DARIN	We rule.
NICK	We own the neighbourhood. (*to the audience*) It never hurts to throw your weight around.
KIM	Mr. Big Shots. Get on with it.
NICK	Right. (*to audience*) Okay, so — I'm not the kind of guy who like wants to get too serious, you know what I mean? Like I like playing, like having fun and this one noon hour, here at the Handy I got sorta carried away, see, and okay I probably shouldn't have — but it turned out pretty amazing. I like — I hate to say this but I like learned something...
OTHERS	(*mock surprise*) He learned something!
NICK	Yeah, and I don't think I would have if I hadn't've gotten carried away like. Anyway I got into trouble for it later, eh? Things catch up sometimes. But okay so that part isn't the important part but... You don't know what I'm talking about, do you? Of course — because

	I'm trying to tell you everything all at once. Slow down, Nick.
OTHERS	Chill, Nick, chill.
NICK	Okay — here's how it goes — like. I'll show you. We were in here — my friends and me...
BILLIE	(*to KIM*) So where's your mother? I'm supposed to pick up a buncha stuff.
KIM	I'll take care of it.
DARIN	Where's your mother, Kimmy Kim Kim? Is she still trying to learn how to speak English?
KIM	(*ignoring him*) What do you want?
BILLIE	(*fishing into pocket*) Just a minute. Don't rush me.
DARIN	It's taking her a long time just to learn English.
KIM	It's hard for her.
BILLIE	Where is it...
NICK	How come you're never in school?
KIM	I'm in school.
NICK	Not very much. You're always working in the shop.
KIM	Just when Mama needs me.
NICK	Mama!

Everybody laughs.

DARIN & BILLIE	Mama, Mama.

NICK	So are you going to school this aft?
KIM	If she gets back. She's at Immigration.
DARIN	Immigration.
KIM	They always take a long time. She never knows whether they'll even see her.
BILLIE	What's Immigration?
KIM	She's trying to make sure we can stay in Canada.
BILLIE	Aw, as if, as if! Come on. Nobody's going to make you leave if you don't want to.
KIM	It happens. I thought you wanted to buy something.
BILLIE	(*still searching*) Can't find the list. My mother's going to kill me.
DARIN	My dad says we don't need any more people in the country. They take jobs away from real people. Gimme a bag of chips, okay? Regular.
NICK	You can be so nice, Darin.
KIM	(*giving him the chips*) Seventy five cents.
DARIN	(*as he pays*) I didn't say it. My dad did.
KIM	(*pointing to a piece of paper on the floor*) What's that?
BILLIE	(*picking it up*) How did that happen? (*handing it over*) Here.
KIM	(*reading*) Milk, butter — back there in the cooler.

> *BILLIE goes off. KIM tries to read the rest of the note.*

KIM	I can't—
DARIN	You can't read English either? Lemme see. (*puzzling over it and then to NICK*) You read it.
NICK	Fettucine Alfredo.
DARIN	(*wrinkling his nose*) What's that?
KIM	Italian. (*he goes off to find it*) It'll be near the Tortellini...
NICK	Heeeey! (*to the audience*) I finally saw it. Something new had been moved in — right between the magazine rack and the Frito Chip rack. It was covered with a plastic sheet and it was big and it wasn't the right shape for a milk cooler or anything like that. (*to DARIN*) Do you see what I see?
DARIN	Like, am I blind?
NICK	There's something awesome under that sheet.
DARIN	Awesome.
NICK	Are you thinking what I'm thinking?
DARIN	ESP, man. I'm cool. It's gotta be a —
NICK	Yeah?
DARIN	It could only be a —
NICK	Yeah?
DARIN	It IS a —
TOGETHER	Yeah!

NICK	(*calling*) Billie! (*to the audience*) The Handy had sprung for a Video Game Machine! (*to KIM*). Hey, Kim, when did this arrive?
KIM	What?
DARIN	The Vid Machine, Bright One.
KIM	Oh, that. This morning.
BILLIE	Oh, wow.
KIM	It's just to try out. We probably won't keep it.
NICK	Why not? This is the greatest. Put more in. Turn the place into an arcade. You'd make more money at this than stupid old groceries. (*aside*) It just turns out I'm the greatest of all video game operators. Like I can really do it. I practise at home for hours — you know — like on our Nintendo but nothing beats a real arcade game, right? (*to KIM*) So like turn it on.
KIM	I don't know how.
BILLIE	Which game is it?
KIM	How am I supposed to know?
DARIN	Well it's easy to find out.
NICK	(*aside*) So Darin pulls off the sheet —
KIM	Hey!
ALL	(*simultaneously*) I don't believe it. Fantastic. Totally correct, man. Like amazing. Deadly.

NICK   Beautiful. "War Is Hell!" It was the most beautiful arcade game I'd ever seen and I couldn't wait to play it.

DARIN   There's gotta be a switch or something?

BILLIE   Might help if we plugged it in. Bright, guys, really bright.

Starting to plug it in.

KIM   Let's wait till my mother gets back.

DARIN   Don't be a nerd.

KIM   Something might go wrong.

BILLIE   What could go wrong?

BILLIE succeeds in plugging in the cord and suddenly the machine begins to blare out martial music with realistic sounds of explosions and machine gun fire. KIM turns pale and backs away from the game. The others are fascinated.

MACHINE   The War Machine. Come and play if you dare. Are you man enough to sit in the cockpit of an F18 fighter attack plane? Are you brave enough to fly a Stealth Bomber through deadly tracer fire? Are you fast enough to fire your sidewinder rocket before the enemy shoots you down in flames. Fight in the trenches, endure the hell of naval warfare. Try the War Machine and die. First a short demonstration.

An improvised demonstration with the actors flying around the stage demonstrating a tank and air battle.

NICK (*to the audience*) The screen filled up with like a tank battalion thundering toward us blasting away with those big guns, everything all light and fire — and then we're inside one of the tanks looking out through narrow slits in the armour — and then we're standing on the deck of a destroyer watching a fighter plane coming down right for us — strafing us with machine gun fire — and then suddenly we're right in the plane — and the sea and the ships are coming up to meet us — and then the plane pulls up so fast my stomach starts to feel funny — and all you can see is the sky and the sun blazing and a cloud getting bigger and bigger as we climb until we're surrounded by the mist and then there's a missile coming right for us and a blaze of red fire and smoke and the plane is falling apart around us. The screen goes dark — and then it says...

MACHINE Deposit twenty five cents and press the red button to begin.

DARIN Me first! Me first!

BILLIE No me. I made it work!

NICK What about me. I'm the expert.

DARIN Big deal. I've got the quarter.

He inserts money into the machine. He operates the levers and buttons while NICK describes what happens.

NICK Little Darin gets into his tank.

BILLIE Tikititi—kititik. Slams hatch.

NICK Klang. Starts up engine.

BILLIE RRRRRRRoar. Moves across terrain.

NICK	Sights enemy plane...
DARIN	Fires at enemy plane. Kablam!
NICK	Misses.
DARIN	Shoot.
BILLIE	Enemy plane fires at little Darin. Kablam.
NICK	Little Darin dead.
DARIN	Gets second chance. Tikitititititi—tik
NICK	Klang.
BILLIE	Rrrrrrrooooooaaaar.
NICK	Starts moving across terrain.
BILLIE	Enemy plane approaches.
NICK	Fires.
DARIN	Misses!
BILLIE	Rocket approaches.
DARIN	No no no no —
BILLIE	Kablam!
NICK & BILLIE	Little Darin dead.
BILLIE	Poor little Darin.
DARIN	Third chance.
BILLIE	Final chance

DARIN	Tikititktitktitktitkt.
NICK	Kablam.
DARIN	No fair!! I didn't even get into my tank.
MACHINE	Sorry. War is Hell. Care to try again?
DARIN	I don't have any money left.
MACHINE	Sorry. War is Hell. Care to try again?
NICK	Okay, let an expert take over.
BILLIE	Oh no, if you get on it I'll never get a chance — you'll be on it forever. And I have to take these groceries home before the bell rings. C'mon Nick, c'mon —
NICK	Alright, alright.
BILLIE	(*to KIM*) Do I get any change?
KIM	Twenty cents.
NICK	Don't look at me. All I've got is enough for one game.
BILLIE	Go ahead then.
NICK	Alright! (*contrite*) Sorry, Billie. (*approaching the machine like a champion*) Make way for the Marines! (*to the audience*) Okay so, this was a truly threatening game. That didn't stop me from getting through level one and level two without any problems. I was just too fast for them — pow pow pow pow. Kill, kill, kill.

Sound of a plane approaching.

Oh, no. They're after me.

The others join in.

BILLIE
& DARIN   Kill, kill, kill, kill, kill!

Loud explosion.

NICK   Got him!

The others groan.

BILLIE   I could have done that.

DARIN   Oh yeah?

BILLIE   Sure.

NICK   The explosions on this game were the most realistic I'd ever seen. Level Two was a naval battle — with torpedo hits and ships blowing apart — bits of metal debris and smoke and fire all over the place, bodies flying through the air — enemy sailors drowning in the water — it was magnificent. I didn't make that many points — but still by the end of the level I had one extra life to use if I needed it.

MACHINE   You have had success, you puny wretch. But now you face the full fury of my forces. Prepare for the mother of all battles. Hahahaha!

BILLIE   See, I told you once you got on you'd never get off.

NICK   The original vidkid.

BILLIE   If I don't get home with this stuff I'm dead meat.

BILLIE exits reluctantly.

MACHINE	Listen carefully, Player. Death is on its way. How will it come? In a ball of flame as your aircraft plummets from the sky? Or will you be strafed by deadly canon fire as you eject from the cockpit. Perhaps you will reach the ground only to be captured by my forces. Then death will come slowly and with great agony and you will wish you had never been born. Why not admit defeat now —
NICK	No way!
MACHINE	Because however it comes — one thing is certain — death is coming and you are its target.
NICK	Oh yeah?
MACHINE	To begin the air campaign press the start button.
	The machine sounds enter the wait mode suspenseful and taunting.
DARIN	The bell's going to ring in a minute. We'd better get back into the yard, right?
NICK	(*considering his strategy*) In a minute. In a minute.
MACHINE	Begin by pressing "start".
KIM	I think you better stop playing.
NICK	Why?
KIM	I don't like it, that's all.
DARIN	(*sarcastic*) Kim doesn't like it, Nick. You'd better shut it down. It's too scary for him.
KIM	Take a hike.
DARIN	Oh oh!

MACHINE	Begin by pressing "start".
NICK	I've already got one free battle, Kim. I'm not going to waste this game.

Bell rings in distance.

DARIN	First bell, Nick.
NICK	Shh.
DARIN	If you're late you're going to be in big trouble.
NICK	Say I'm sick or something.
DARIN	Tell them yourself. (*exit*)
KIM	Please?
NICK	Forget it.
KIM	Have it your way, then.

KIM walks away from him.

MACHINE	Begin by pressing "start".
NICK	Okay, so am I ready? Yes! I am ready. (*pressing a button*) Let the Air War begin.

Electronic sounds. Cast is in battle formation. At director's discretion some of the following lines may be divided internally among the actors, overlapped, or spoken in chorus. In the original production, the game was brought to life both with group choreography and with hand movements — much as children will sometimes use their whole bodies and sometimes just their hands to mimic airplanes or rockets.

BILLIE	Your mission will be to fly to co-ordinate two seven two oh...
DARIN	To deposit ordinance consisting of
KIM	Paveway II laser-guided Smart Bombs.
BILLIE	GBU-15 Smart Bombs.
DARIN	AGM-45 Shrike missiles.
KIM	AGM-62 Walleye bombs and Rockeye cluster bombs.
BILLIE	AGM-65 Maverick missiles.
DARIN	AGM-88 Harm missiles.
KIM	On your way to the target you will encounter enemy fighter planes...
BILLIE	Air to air missiles...
DARIN	Surface to air missiles...
KIM	And anti-aircraft artillery fire.
BILLIE	If you complete your mission...
NICK	What do you mean "if"?
DARIN	And drop your ordinance precisely on target.
KIM	You will receive 50,000 points.
NICK	What am I flying? What am I flying?
BILLIE	A state of the art, F-117A Stealth Fighter.
NICK	(*awestruck*) Lethal.

DARIN	Sinister, sleek black metal, all angles...

KIM	Like no other plane in the sky.

NICK	I'm strapped in. The cockpit full of monitors and flashing lights — video screen in my helmet — I feel like I'm inside a computer. All systems checked. Ready to go.

BILLIE	Then fly.

Tremendous roar as the plane takes off.

DARIN	I'm bringing up three aircraft on radar approaching at high speed. Repeat, three bogies on an intercept course.

KIM	Three MIg's diving down towards you out of the sun.

BILLIE	Cannons are firing, radar's locked on, their missiles at launch ready.

NICK	(*working his controls furiously*) I blanket the air in front of me with cannon fire. I get a fix on two of the MIg's one after the other and launch sidewinders. I manoeuver between them firing all the time. I can feel the heat and the concussion as the missiles hit — one...

Explosion.

Two...

Explosion.

DARIN	But the third one has looped and now he's on your tail.

NICK	I ease up all of a sudden — braking action — and drop. He'll fly past me — I'll get him with another sidewinder.

Explosion.

Home-free.

KIM — Enemy aircraft scrambling from hidden runways below you. Ten fighters rising to meet you.

NICK — Speed up. Drop some bombs on them. Out manoeuver them. Out gun them. Out race them.

BILLIE — Ground to air missiles are being launched. A wall of steel.

DARIN — You'll never get through.

KIM — You're finished.

NICK — Wanna bet? I blast through the rising missiles weaving and turning explosions and fire all around me and finally I'm through the danger zone...

BILLIE — Fuel warning! Fuel warning. You are dangerously low on fuel.

NICK — But the target is on the horizon.

DARIN — Anti-aircaft artillery lights up the sky like fireworks — a curtain of blue flame dead ahead...

NICK — I pull... pull back on the joy stick, sending her into a climb — straight up like a rocket reaching for the stars... up out of artillery range...

Roar of the engine.

KIM — Your starboard engine stalls —

NICK — Oh no...

KIM — You lose way —

NICK   I loop and send the plane into a dive — maybe I can start the engine, start, damn you — start!

Sound of a plane diving — engine suddenly restored.

BILLIE   You have full power. You have full power...

NICK   I pull up again...

DARIN   You can't pull up without flying through tracer fire.

NICK   Too late — I'm into it....

KIM   Target area in range...

BILLIE   More surface to air missiles approaching...

NICK   I see the target — I see the target...

DARIN   MIg 32 on your tail.

The noise and excitement is reaching an almost unbearable crescendo.

NICK   I've got a laser lock on it!

KIM   (*breaking out of the game*) No, stop it! Stop it!

NICK   Bombs away! I've won! I've won!

Sounds of bombs falling — but before the inevitable detonation KIM pulls the plug on the machine. BILLIE and DARIN back out of the action and the stage is in stark silence. NICK is left furiously jerking at the dead controls. Finally he gives it a vicious kick. He looks up to see a trembling KIM with the plug in his hand.

NICK   What did you do that for?

> *KIM can't speak.*

NICK: I was so close. I've never done that well ever — I might have gotten to the top level.

> *He paces up and down, hitting and kicking things, trying to work off his anger. The aggression built by the video game seeks another target.*

I could have made it, you know. I could have. What's wrong with you? You don't just pull the plug in the middle of a game. You don't do that!

KIM: (*almost to himself*) No game.

NICK: What? (*no response*) What did you say?

KIM: No game.

NICK: Right, no game. Not now. Why don't you just — why don't you just go back where you came from?

KIM: (*flaring*) And where do you think that is?

NICK: How should I know?

KIM: Right — how should you know? You couldn't care less, right?

NICK: Right.

KIM: (*pointing at the machine*) That's where I came from.

NICK: (*mystified*) What?

KIM: That's where I came from.

NICK: In there? Don't / be stupid.

KIM (*speaking at the / in previous line*) No! I mean where the bombs are falling. That's where I came from. I was there — on the ground when the planes flew over and dropped their bombs — not in there — for real. My mom and me — we're refugees.

NICK Refugees.

KIM You don't know what refugees are?

NICK Of course I know what refugees are. In a way. I mean, like if you want an exact definition...

KIM People trying to find a place that's safe. People running away from war.

NICK Right. (*pause*) You were in a war?

KIM busies himself with store items.

Were you?

KIM Yeah.

NICK Really.

KIM Yeah. Really.

NICK What was it like?

KIM Shouldn't you get back to class or something?

NICK I'm already in big trouble. A little more won't hurt — much. Tell me.

KIM What?

NICK About the war.

KIM I don't want to talk about it.

NICK	Aw — c'mon. Did you see any bombs? (*to the audience*) You know, like I was excited. I'd never talked to anybody who'd been in a war before. (*to KIM*) So, like — what's it like?

He doesn't answer.

Really — what's it like?

KIM	Figure it out yourself.
NICK	Is it exciting? Did you ever see any — rockets — machine guns — what? Have you ever been near where a bomb fell?
KIM	Yeah.

NICK turns to the audience.

NICK	He started to talk. I don't know what got him started. Maybe because I was being such a — like actually I can't think of a polite way to say it. Anyway he started to talk and I guess he told me a lot more than I wanted to hear.
KIM	The first time — I don't know how old I was. (*sighs*) I was just little — I think it might have been the first time our town was hit. I heard this big noise and I didn't know what it was.
NICK	What where you doing — when it — when it hit?
KIM	Playing. In the front of our house — with the other kids.
NICK	What were you playing?
KIM	What difference does it make?
NICK	I want to know everything.

KIM		I told you I was just little — I don't remember. Yes I do! We were playing Cowboys and Indians.
NICK		No! really?
KIM		Yes, really.
NICK		How did you know about Cowboys and Indians?
KIM		Old movies, how else? How did you know about Cowboys and Indians?
NICK		Old movies.
KIM		Right.
NICK		So you were playing Cowboys and Indians...

BILLIE enters as KIM's playmate. They are firing imaginary carbines at one another and whooping it up.

KIM   And then there was this blast...

Sound of an explosion.

And the ground shook. My father came out of the house and we ran to him.

DARIN takes on the role of KIM's father. As he runs to him another explosion is heard. KIM puts his fingers in his ears. The other child huddles with them.

We could see smoke climbing into the air on the other side of the village. (*to DARIN*) What is it, Papa?

BILLIE   Make it stop.

KIM   What is it?

DARIN	Shh. Don't be afraid. Stop crying and I'll tell you what I think is happening.
KIM	I've stopped.
DARIN	Are you sure?
KIM	I'm sure.
BILLIE	What is it?
DARIN	I think it's somebody burping.
KIM	(*laughing in spite of his fear*) Burping.
DARIN	That's right. That big fat old fellow who lives near the market, maybe.
KIM	I never heard anybody burp that loud.
BILLIE	Me neither.
DARIN	Now that I think of it — I'm sure that's what happened. The man loves cabbages. I saw him at the market and I told him — Yosef, I said — one day you will eat too many cabbages, I said — and you'll come out with the biggest belch — you'll make the ground shake for miles around — and you might even burst — like a big balloon...
	Sound of planes in the distance fading away. Everyone looks up.
KIM	And in the sky there were long vapour trails left by jets flying so high we couldn't even see them.
DARIN	Bring me your brother's field glasses, Son.
KIM	My older brother had been given a pair of binoculars for his birthday.

> *DARIN as the father picks up a pair of field glasses from a shelf. He raises them to his eyes and looks into the sky. There is a long pause.*

KIM (*finally*) What do you see, Papa?

BILLIE Bang, bang. You're dead!

KIM I'm not dead. You're dead.

DARIN Into the house now. Time for bed.

> *Chorus of "Aww — it's still early — do we have to?" etc.*

Off you go.

BILLIE (*leaving sadly*) Bye.

DANIEL (*cutting short further protest from KIM*) Now!

> *Everyone moves off to one side as if going inside a cottage. KIM and NICK break out of the group.*

KIM My father — he had a certain tone of voice sometimes and when he used that tone of voice — we all jumped. But really he wouldn't hurt a fly. He was funny, and kind of gentle...

NICK Was?

KIM Is — used to be. Anyway (*plunging ahead*) about the bombs.

NICK Yeah, about the bombs.

KIM That first time, they said, was just a warning. We didn't understand that. Something to do with politics. What do little kids know about politics, right? The first year — the bombing wasn't heavy — we got used to it — sometimes there was nothing for months — and life was normal — people worked their farms — you know — raised their crops and sold them in the markets. We went to school — and sometimes we even hoped there'd be an air raid so we'd get out of math — but not really. You always felt just a little bit afraid.

NICK   I wouldn't've.

KIM   Yes, you would've. (*pause*) When the bombs were falling, I'd be shaking I was so scared. Once a bomb blew the side of our house in. I was inside — another two meters maybe, I would have been killed. After that I had bad dreams — a lot of bad dreams. I'd wake up screaming in the night. (*screaming*) No, no, no! Leave me alone! Why are they doing this to us? We never hurt them!!

    DARIN and BILLIE rush to him as his parents.

BILLIE   Kim, Kim. It's alright. It's alright. Be calm — we're here.

KIM   Stay with me. Stay here.

DARIN   Don't be afraid, Kim. Don't be afraid. We're not going any place. We'll always be here.

KIM   Why did he make that promise to me? Why?

BILLIE   Go back to sleep now.

KIM   I can't. I'm scared.

DARIN   Of those fellows? We don't have to be scared of those fellows.

KIM   Why not?

DARIN   Why not? Because they are so scared of us!

KIM   Of us?

DARIN   Of course. Why do you think they come here with their bombs and their rockets?

KIM   Because they hate us.

DARIN   No — because they're terrified! They know we don't have any planes or bazookas or anything — but they're still so scared they bring along all that heavy equipment. Maybe it's because I'm so ugly looking — what do you think?

BILLIE   That must be it, then...

DARIN   Hey!

BILLIE   Makes perfect sense to me.

DARIN   All the time she disagrees with me. Now I say I'm ugly and she agrees right away.

KIM   And they laughed and I laughed and I went back to sleep again.

He hands NICK the field glasses.

My brother. Once my brother and me hiked out of town to this place we used to go.

NICK hesitates and then takes on the character of KIM's brother. He absently begins to look around with the field glasses taking his cues from KIM.

KIM   Our town was in a valley and there were mountains on all sides. And we could stand on this hill and look up into the mountains — and this day we could see things happening on the slopes.

NICK	(*handing him the binoculars*) Hey, look.
KIM	(*to NICK*) All those flashes...little puffs of smoke...
NICK	They're fighting up there. Listen —
KIM	I don't hear anything. (*pause*) Oh — now I do. Like little firecrackers or something.
NICK	I can see — I can see people running down the trails — they've got rifles. I wish I was up there...
KIM	(*breaking out of role*) That's not what he said. (*changing subject*) You know something? If you're out in the open and bombs are falling where do you think is safest place to be?
NICK	I don't know — behind a tree or something?
KIM	On top of a hill.
NICK	Why?
KIM	Because the bomb might fall down the side and explode away from you. Maybe.
NICK	Maybe.
KIM	You know something else?
NICK	(*subdued*) What?
KIM	If a rocket missile is coming at you — it can explode before you hear the sound of its engine.
NICK	Why?
KIM	'Cause it goes faster than sound. (*pause*) You don't know what hit you. You're just dead.

NICK	Oh.
KIM	Things you learn in a war. Like how people look when they've been blown apart — and like how dead bodies smell — and the sound tanks make in the main street — and what happens if you go out at night after curfew. You get shot, that's all. And you learn to be afraid when a knock comes at the door. You never know what they'll do to you. I hate them. I hate the people that are doing this to us.
DARIN	(*as the father*) Don't hate. Try not to hate. They're just humans like us. Stand proud — be proud of who you are. But don't hate.
KIM	I couldn't believe my father. The things he told us. Maybe it was to keep us safe. When the soldiers came it was better to pretend you liked them. Once I saw a tank run some kids down — just because they threw stones at it. Stones! How could they hurt a tank with a few little stones. The treads crushed their—

NICK turns away.

KIM	Had enough?
NICK	Go on.
KIM	Okay, Bomber Pilot.

This hurts but NICK doesn't say anything.

They started to arrest people in the town — on suspicion of being against them — of helping their enemies... men — even boys — even —

BILLIE and DARIN take on the roles of soldiers. They bang at a door.

BILLIE	Open up. Open up, in there.

DARIN	Do you hear us? Listen, kid — open the door.
BILLIE	You don't want us to break it down, do you?
DARIN	What would your parents say?
KIM	I'm coming...

He opens a door and the soldiers burst through.

BILLIE	(*seeing KIM*) It's just the little one.
DARIN	Where's your brother, Kid?
KIM	I don't know. He's out in the country.
DARIN	(*to the others*) Look around.

They start searching, trashing a few things in the process.

KIM	You shouldn't do that.
BILLIE	Who says?
KIM	My parents...
BILLIE	Your parents aren't here — so you just stay back. Do what we tell you and we'll be real nice.
DARIN	(*picking up the binoculars*) Who do these belong to?
KIM	My brother... (*to NICK*) As soon as the words were out of my mouth I knew it was the wrong thing to say — if I'd only lied about it...
BILLIE	Your brother —
DARIN	What does he use them for?

BILLIE	Watching us, maybe?
DARIN	Identifying aircraft?
BILLIE	Picking out troop movements?
DARIN	Spying?
BILLIE	Speak up, kid. Speak up!
KIM	He doesn't use them for anything. Just for fun.
DARIN	Fun!
KIM	Yes, Sir.
BILLIE	He likes fun, does he?
KIM	I guess so.
DARIN	Well, maybe we can give him a little.
BILLIE	Yeah, we like fun too.

They leave with the binoculars.

KIM They picked him up when he was coming back from the market place. He had a bag of oranges and they took it away from him — made him climb up into the back of a truck with a bunch of others from our town. They drove them south to the city and threw them in prison. My father was called to go there one night — he had a few words with my brother and then that same night — they — they — took him — they hanged him. They — they sent my father a bill for shipping his body home and the coffin. I saw his body before the funeral — it was all blue and twisted. I could see where the rope had been around his neck...

NICK No.

DARIN	(*as Father*) You and your mother will get away from this place.
BILLIE	(*as Mother*) But where — where can we go?
DARIN	We have the money we've saved — perhaps you can go as far as America or Canada. Go as far away from here as you can — somewhere you will be safe. Somewhere you can go to school and not be afraid of a bomb blowing up your classroom.
KIM	You, Papa — what will you do?
DARIN	I will go into the mountains with the others — I'll fight...
KIM	My mother screamed and threw herself down at his knees. I cried and hung on his arm.
BILLIE	And what of your fine talk of peace and not hating anyone? This is against everything you believe!
KIM	He was a kind person — not even very strong. He'd hate fighting —
DARIN	I know — I'll hate it. I'm not sure I'll even be any good at it — but what can I do. They've killed my son! Why should they get away with it?
BILLIE	Even if you get killed too?
KIM	Papa?
DARIN	This is the way war goes. Once it starts — it goes on like this... Nobody's life is important anymore — not even your own.
KIM	We left under cover of the night — it was the last we saw of him... Look — here are some pictures.

> *KIM takes some snapshots out from behind the counter and passes them to NICK who looks at them almost reverently.*

NICK Is that your mother? She looks — she looks so —

KIM She looks young in the picture — and now she looks like an old lady?

> *NICK doesn't want to speak.*

It's true. She got old all of a sudden. (*abruptly showing him another snapshot*) This is our house before the bomb hit...

NICK Looks nice.

KIM (*another snapshot*) And after.

NICK Gross.

KIM (*another snapshot*) My cousins — we think they managed to get to France or someplace — we don't know where exactly. (*another snapshot*) My brother.

NICK With the field glasses.

KIM On his birthday.

> *Another snapshot.*

NICK Your father.

> *KIM nods, unable to speak.*

He looks...

KIM Like he wouldn't hurt a fly.

NICK Yeah.

KIM | That's war.

NICK | So... So I can see why you pulled the plug... I guess... (*pause*) But it's only a game...

KIM | Not for me.

NICK | I was just having... fun. What's wrong with that?

KIM shrugs.

KIM | It's okay.

The school bell rings.

NICK | What time is it? (*to the audience*) School was over for the day. I hadn't even heard the recess bell. I couldn't believe it. I'd spent the whole afternoon in the store.

Enter BILLIE and DARIN.

BILLIE | Oh, oh Nicky!! Are you ever going to get it.

DARIN | You're in trouble, Nicky boy.

BILLIE | Deep, deep trouble.

DARIN | Old lady Millstead called your house. Nobody was at home.

BILLIE | Old man Anderson asked the class if anybody had seen you.

NICK | What did you guys say?

DARIN | Nothin'.

BILLIE | Nothin'.

DARIN   'Cept we'd heard there was a new video game in the neighbourhood.

KIM   Some friends.

DARIN   Us?

KIM   Bozos.

BILLIE   Look who's calling us names!

DARIN   You ever heard the names they call you people? You want to hear a few? Do you? Do you?

NICK   Leave him alone.

BILLIE   What have you been doing all afternoon, Nick?

NICK   Playing the machine.

BILLIE   On one quarter? Sure, Nicky, sure.

DARIN   What level did you get to, Nicky?

BILLIE   So if you played the machine all afternoon how come it's shut off, eh?

NICK   It was just—

KIM   I shut it off.

BILLIE   Why?

NICK   He had to, that's all.

BILLIE   Because the machine was driving you crazy, right?

DARIN   You were losing all your money, right?

BILLIE   You were coming up zilch, zero, nada — right?

NICK	We were talking.
DARIN	All afternoon? Sure, Nick.
BILLIE	Nico. (*pulling a quarter out of her pocket*) What do you think this says?
NICK	It says you found a quarter.
BILLIE	This says I can make three times as many points as you did.
NICK	On that game?
BILLIE	Of course.
NICK	No way, man. I practically beat the machine. I went through all the lines of defence. I found the target — I let go my bombs and that's when... (*he suddenly looks at KIM and breaks off*)
BILLIE	When what?
NICK	So there's no way you can beat my score.
BILLIE	Just watch me.

She tries to get at the machine.

DARIN	So what was your score?
NICK	I'm not sure. You think I had time to look?

NICK is blocking BILLIE's access to the game. At first it seems like he is joking but NICK is resolved to keep them from turning it on.

BILLIE	Get out of my way, Nick. C'mon — get out of my way. What's wrong? Afraid I'll beat you? You're chicken, eh? Eh? Eh? Cluck cluck cluck!

She tries to deke around him several times.

NICK Fast. (*blocking again and again*) But not fast enough.

DARIN joins in.

DARIN Afraid you'll get shown up, Nicky?

NICK Why don't you go down to the arcade and play?

BILLIE I want to play this one.

DARIN And so do I.

NICK I can handle ten squirts like you.

BILLIE Look who's calling who a squirt. Get him, Dar.

NICK No you don't.

NICK grabs them both by the shirts and there is a lot of pushing and shoving. The mood begins to turn a little ugly.

DARIN Hey, that hurt!

NICK You think that hurt...

DARIN Get him, Billie...

NICK Shut up, Snot Head...

BILLIE Grab his leg...

NICK You want a kick in the face...?

KIM Nick. Nick!

The three fighters pause in surprise.

KIM   It's not worth fighting over.

                 He plugs it in for them. The machine lights up and plays its introductory sounds.

MACHINE   The War Machine. Come and play if you dare. Are you man enough to sit in the cockpit of / an F18 fighter attack plane? Are you brave enough to fly a Stealth Bomber through deadly tracer fire? Are you fast enough to fire your cruise missile, your sidewinder rocket before the enemy shoots you down in flames. You may also engage in trench warfare or a tank battle. It is your choice. Try the War Machine and die. First a short demonstration.

                 The realistic sounds of war continue to build. The following dialogue begins at the "/" above and continues over the sound of the game.

DARIN   (*gaping at the screen again*) That is the best. That is perfect.

BILLIE   Let me at it.

KIM   Let them.

NICK   (*stepping aside*) I thought you said...

KIM   It's okay. Really.

BILLIE   (*to KIM*) You'd better not pull it on me.

KIM   I won't.

DARIN   Go for it. Kill, kill, kill, kill.

BILLIE   The Warrior inserts her Secret identification code.

                 She deposits her quarter.

BILLIE   And the data screen in the cockpit comes to life.

NICK   (*to KIM*) I don't get it. Doesn't this bring everything back all over again.

KIM   We need the customers. That's the whole point of it.

NICK   But, Kim —

KIM   I'll turn it off in my head. I'll try not to hear it. It has nothing to do with me. Nothing to do with me. I'm not even here.

> *As the game warms up BILLIE and DARIN begin to chant again.*

BILLIE
& DARIN   Kill, kill, kill, kill!

NICK   (*shouting over the building sound of war*) Billie! Darin.

BILLIE   Shut up!

> *The chant continues with the war sounds getting heavier. NICK screaming is almost drowned by the noise.*

NICK   Guys — you gotta understand! War is about real people!

BILLIE   What?

> *NICK pulls the plug. The sound stops and everyone's attention is on NICK.*

NICK   War...is about real people.

DARIN   You're weird, man.

BILLIE	If I've lost my quarter, I'm going to kill you, man.
NICK	Can you hear yourself?
DARIN	(*to KIM*) What did you do to him?
KIM	Nothing.
NICK	War is about people like us — being afraid and learning to hate the enemy and getting blown up...
BILLIE	(*enthusiastically*) Alright!
DARIN	Yeah...
BILLIE	So plug it back in.
NICK	And it's about families getting split up and kids escaping and having to work in the corner store and listen to us going crazy over a video game.
KIM	It's okay, Nick.

BILLIE AND DARIN are stopped in their tracks.

Leave it alone, alright?

BILLIE	Kim?
DARIN	What are you trying to say, Nick?
NICK	He went through all that.
BILLY	War?
KIM	Yeah.
DARIN	For real? You were in a war?
BILLY	(*excited*) What was it like?

They gather around KIM at the counter.

NICK — No fun. (*stepping away from the group and addressing the audience*) That's it. That's what happened to me one afternoon at the Handy. And the thing I learned — I guess — like — it's that war isn't just something that happens like on a video screen or TV.

DARIN — Where did you live?

NICK — (*to audience*) It happens in a real place.

BILLIE — (*looking at the photographs on the counter*) Is this your family?

NICK — It happens to real people.

DARIN — Tell us about it.

NICK — And it isn't any fun. These games we play? All the movies we watch about war? They like lie. They lie.

BILLY — Come on, Kim. Tell us about it.

Freeze and break.

The End.

Other published works by Rex Deverell...

"The Copetown City Kite Crisis"
in *Class Acts*, Playwrights Canada Press

"The Riel Commission"
in *Studio One: Stories Made for Radio*, Coteau Books

Deverell of the Globe, NeWest Press.

"Melody Meets the Bag Lady"
in *Eight Plays for Young People*, NeWest Press.

"Medicare"
in *Showing West: Three Prairie Docu-Dramas*, NeWest Press.

Black Powder: Estevan 1931, Coteau Books.

"Switching Places"
in *Eureka*. Coteau Books